spaces

spaces

architecture in detail

edited by oscar riera ojeda

written by james mccown

photography by paul warchol

First published in the United States of America by Rockport Publishers, Inc.
33 Commercial Street
Gloucester, Massachusetts 01930-5089
Telephone: (978) 282-9590
Fax: (978) 283-2742
www.rockpub.com

Library of Congress Cataloging-in-Publication data available.

design and layout by oscar riera ojeda

ISBN 1-59253-106-7

10 9 8 7 6 5 4 3 2 1

Manufactured in China by Max Production Printing & Book Binding Ltd. (Samuel Fung, Managing Director)

Cover photograph: Sam Trimble Architect, Roberts Apartment, New York, 2003. Previous page: Rogers Marvel Architects, Canal Street Residence, New York, 2003. This spread: Steven Holl Architects, Simmons Hall MIT, Cambridge, Massachusetts, 2002. Contents page: Frank Lloyd Wright, Guggenheim Museum, New York, 1959.

Back jacket flap photography credits: portrait of James McCown and Oscar Riera Ojeda © Paul Warchol (top) and Paul Warchol © Abraham Aronow (bottom).

rockport publishers

contents

introduction 8

entry 14   hallway 34   great room 60   bedroom 84   bathroom 100   terrace 124   office 140   retail 156   exhibition 174

acknowledgments & dedications 192

introduction

by james mccown

Friedrich von Schelling's famous quote, "Architecture is frozen music," once drew the retort: "Yes, but music is not melted architecture." ■ Whatever the links between these two great arts, both exist *in time*. Musical notes become a symphony only when they are performed; a building becomes architecture only when we move through it or about it. Imagine the Roman Emperor Justinian in A.D. 537, entering his newly completed Hagia Sophia, commissioned in his capital city of Constantinople. Passing through an inner and outer narthex, intentionally dark and constrictive, he arrives at the central space, under a huge dome seemingly suspended from the sky, light streaming through its circular band of clerestory windows. ■ "Solomon, I have surpassed thee," he says in awe and vanity, having built a monument usurping the Biblical King's temple in Jerusalem. ■ This book is about architectural spaces, both interior and exterior. It may itself seem an act of overreaching vanity to use the august Hagia Sophia to begin a discussion about contemporary architectural spaces. And yet it is procession through spaces that most concerns architects. And that procession is most usually expressed in an enduring architectural element: the room. ■ The room is a human creation. The root of the word is related to the German *Raum* meaning "a place cleared for settlement or lodging." The forming of indoor and outdoor spaces is a primal human activity. Siegfried Giedeon writes: "Man takes cognizance of the emptiness which girds around him and gives it a psychic form and expression . . . [space is] the portrayal of man's inner relation to his environment: man's psychic record of the realities which confront him, which lie about him and

and two rooms *en suite* . . . [a] place for the hearth, followed by the innermost room. The earliest megaron was developed first as a dwelling for humans and later as a temple type for the gods . . . As people moved from the open landscape into the enclosed space of the megaron, the degree of enclosure was varied by a deliberate sequential ordering that created visual and perceptual information and interest. The linking of building and site was accomplished through a logical redimensioning of the landscape and grouping of forms into a whole."[4] ■ Further refining this archetype, in the Classical Greek temple, great care was taken in the sequence that the individual would experience: the stairs leading to the *plinth*, from which an overall vista could be had; a surrounding colonnaded *peristyle*, used often for ritualistic processions; the *pronaos*, an entry room for preparation; and finally the *cella*, the grandest space with high ceilings and usually featuring flanking rows of columns and an effigy of the patron god or goddess. ■ In the Middle Ages and Renaissance, a procession of interior architectural spaces was meant to reflect a divinely sanctioned order of things. In a Gothic cathedral, the entry narthex led to the nave, defined by soaring, pointed arches and lit by multicolored windows. The point above the altar was the penultimate space. The entire assemblage drew the eye ever upward. ■ The paradigm of spatial hierarchy continued through the neoclassical and neo-Gothic eras until the modern era. Among the ideas that were refined: the experience of going from room to room—how a doorway frames the appearance of a hallway ahead in a symmetrical *enfilade*; the subtle change of ceiling

the enduring room

become transformed."[1] Bruno Zevi describes buildings as "hollow sculpture": "Architecture . . . does not consist in the sum of the width, length and height of the structural elements which enclose space, but in the void itself, the closed space in which man lives and moves."[2] ■ As Katherine F. Benzel explains in her book, *The Room in Context*: "The word 'room' is a generic term for a space that is perceived to be closed, such as an office, classroom, hotel lobby, dining room, or picture gallery. Many elements are used . . . high opaque walls to create privacy, encircling colonnades to produce openness, glass walls to connect space inside to space outside, adjustable partitions to create a temporary semiprivate space, nooks and alcoves to serve as corners where we take refuge, and low ridges symbolically separating one space from another."[3] Add to this the much-used reference by architects of exterior spaces whose layout and design make them "outdoor rooms." ■ Benzel discusses the spatial composition of the megaron, the building archetype that emerged in Minoan and Mycenean civilizations around the eighth century B.C.: ". . . the megaron had three divisions: the front entry

heights; the experience of rising through space on a curved stairway. ■ In the nineteenth-century *Beaux-Arts* school, spatial order and sequence were given primary importance. Public and civic structures from city halls to banks to libraries and courthouses had elaborate series of rotunda, anterooms and chambers. Occupants were directed through highly formal and ritualistic groupings of rooms meant by extension to suggest the order and harmony of civilized urban life. The entry staircase was especially important in museums because of the implied metaphor of rising to be edified by great artwork. ■ Emerging in the period between the World Wars, modernists such as Le Corbusier and Mies van der Rohe cared little for the hierarchy of a pompous state apparatus or a discredited aristocracy. For them, the very notion of a staid demarcation of rooms needed to be rethought completely. The result was the *plan libre*. Zevi discusses: ". . . supporting pillars are raised from the foundation to the roof before any interior or exterior walls are put up . . . Using vast windows, by now entire walls of glass, [there is] complete continuity between interior and exterior space.

Internal wall partitions, which no longer work with static bearing functions, may now be thin, curved, freely movable. This creates the possibility of linking up interior spaces, of . . . the open and elastic plan of modern building."[5] Specific to Mies, Franz Schulze writes: ". . . he sought to explore the dynamism of space by breaking down barriers between interior space and exterior space [figure 1] and by relating interior spaces more closely to each other. Glass and freestanding walls become his primary means of achieving these ends . . .."[6] ■ In the United States, throughout his career Frank Lloyd Wright undertook a reconceptualizing of space [figure 2], as described by Charles Riley: "Wright conceived of his architecture in its essence as a revolt against 'enclosure,' a way to 'beat the box,' as he put it . . . [the interiors] flowed from living area to dining area and beyond, removing the walls that created interior boxes. Wright called this 'the liberation of space to space.' The apotheosis of this liberation is the nearly seamless transition from interior to exterior . . .."[7] ■ As change swirled around, other early twentieth-century phenomena were profoundly affecting the building art. Photography had freed the artist from having to create approximations of real life, and the newer art of cinema was completely redefining human perception through the dynamism of space and the spatialization of time. Andres Janser quotes Giedion as believing passionately that the two emerging art forms—film and modern architecture—were naturally allied: "Still photography does not capture [modern buildings] clearly. One would have to accompany the eye as it moves: only film can make

before: "Imagine . . . that you are in your living room at eight o'clock in the evening. One window on your computer screen connects you to a database on which you are paid to work, another shows the news from CNN, and another puts you in a digital chat room . . . Children come and go, making their usual demands. Are you at work or at play?"[9] Of the increasingly evident media rooms and other electronic accouterments, Mitchell states: "Such presents itself as hearth that radiates information instead of heat. Just as the fireplace with its chimney and mantel was the focus of a traditional living room . . . the source of data, news, and entertainment now bids to become the most powerful organizer of domestic space and activities."[10] ■ With the great changes in technology and evolution of ideas about work, home and leisure, architects are responding in innovative ways in crafting rooms. At the Rosenthal Center for Contemporary Art in Cincinnati [pages 42–45], Zaha Hadid has dispensed with the *Beaux-Arts* idea of stairs, now increasingly problematic because of physical accessibility requirements. But in her choices of placement and materials, she has also blurred the line between inside and out, attempting to turn the lobby into a continuation of the city's sidewalks. ■ The building exterior's aggressively extruded cubes [figure 3] thrust toward the street, some arresting their motion early, others continuing to form overhang and protective exterior canopies. Inside, a central organizing stair seems to float unsupported [figure 4], and patrons move up or through walls and other planes at obtuse angles. The architect calls it "a journey of compression,

1   2   3   4

the new architecture intelligible!"[8] In the early 1930s, Le Corbusier collaborated on a film entitled *Architectures d'aujourd'hui*. In his iconic Villa Savoye, a woman is shown rising up the structure's central organizing ramp, taking in the interplay of solids and voids and different vistas as she approaches the roof terrace. ■ Today, this experience could be replicated not only in a video but in a building that does not yet exist. Programs such as 3D Studio and VIZ allow architects and their clients to imagine how a space will flow before concrete is mixed or a single nail is hit. The software features virtual cameras that allow the user to take up a multiple number of positions to "walk through" or "fly over" buildings. The invention of linear perspective in the early Renaissance changed architecture forever, and the impact of the computer on the art and profession of building is equally far-reaching. ■ MIT professor William J. Mitchell holds forth on both the perils and promises of technology in our homes and workplaces. He points out that Lewis Mumford's contention of "the gradual divorce of the home . . . from the workplace" has in fact been reversed. The two merge as never

release and reflection."[11] Both client and architect wanted to use the building as a symbolic structure, especially in the wake of racial unrest in one of the city's neighborhoods. Thus the city's grid is subtly "fractured" by the architectural intervention. "Here is a place that values experiment, innovation and diversity," wrote the museum director of the ideas that drove the design. For her part, Hadid adds, provocatively: "Neutral space is a wishful oxymoron." ■ The combination of powefull computer modeling and greater daring structural systems allows architects to recall and replicate tectonic shifts in the earth's surface. Note the colliding prominent forms of Weiss/Manfredi's Museum of the Earth in Ithaca, New York [figure 5]. In responding to the hilly, glacially-formed site, the rooms appear to converge toward a single point, suggesting compressive terrestrial forces. The various outdoor spaces are compelling, as well. Angular roof planes [figure 6] form wonderful, almost geological spaces under and among the buildings. ■ The influence of modern painters Piet Mondrian and Theo van Doesburg's on architectural spatial concepts continues to be felt. As if to up-end their contemporaries' concepts of architectural space, the modern masters tried to reduce space to a flat-plane essence, a reductive world of primary colors with geometric shapes organized by black lines. Carel Blotkamp quotes Mondrian: "The new vision . . . does not proceed from a fixed point. Its viewpoint is everywhere, and not limited to any one position. Nor is it bound by space or time [in accordance with the theory of relativity]. In practice, the viewpoint is in front of the plane. Thus this new vision sees architecture as a multiplicity of planes: again flat. This multiplicity composes itself [in an abstract sense] into a flat image."[12] ■ The Mondrianesque façades of Peter Marino + Assoc Architects' Chanel stores [pages 168-171], located in New York, Paris and other cities, seem at once to be reductive exercises in geometrics as well as attempts to blur the distinction between building and billboard. The elegant black grid is glazed with panels of carbon fiber, gold leaf, poured resin and glass fiber. Inside, black-framed doors and partitions organize the space. From the street, the illuminated panels appear to change subtly and are animated by shadows passing within the interior. Using Coco Chanel's aphorism, "Fashion is architecture. It's all a matter of proportion" as a starting point, Marino states: "From inception, the Chanel look has been very modern, from the cut of the clothing to the packaging's crisp geometric forms and defining black outlines."[13] So in deconstructing the boundary between architecture and advertising, Marino also subverts the modernist notion of architecture as being fully detached from the vagaries of fashion. ■ In a more private realm, Peter Gluck's Fowler

Mies and Gordon Bunshaft, is at once celebrated and mocked. ■ The architecture of work, home and play is fraught with contention. As far back as 1927, a Dadaesque work by Marcel Duchamp, *Door: 11, rue Larrey, Paris* satirized the notion of privacy: To shut the door on the bedroom is to open it on the bathroom, and vice versa. Bill Arning discusses another absurdist work, this one by René Magritte: ". . . in *Lunette d'Approche* of 1963, a window reveals a beautiful blue sky through its glass panes, but it is open slightly and in the gap we see pitch blackness, a palpable nothingness . . . The sense [is] that walls keep secrets, which can be literally revealed by violating their seeming immutability."[15] ■ Substantial work has been done over the past thirty years on the subject of architectural space and gender. Just as men's and women's childhood experiences and physiognomies are different, so are the realms they inhabit: "Men rule the outside, women the inside."[16] In a less politically correct time, great buildings were most often described in masculine terms. L.K. Weisman identifies a priapic quote from Louis Sullivan regarding a building by his contemporary Henry Hobson Richardson: "Here is a man for you to look at, a virile force, an entire male. It stands in physical fact, a monument to trade, to the organized commercial spirit, to the power and progress of the age, to the strength and resource of individuality and force of character. Therefore I have called it, in a world of barren prettiness, a male, for it sings the song of procreant power, as others have squealed of miscegenation."[17] ■ Men and women have developed different roles within the

Residence in New Canaan, Connecticut has been dubbed locally "the crate and barrel." The house's program is separated between two wings, one a box and the other a cylinder [figure 7]. In addition to yielding dramatic, circular interior spaces [figure 8], this latter wing has a purposeful rupture that evokes Gordon Matta-Clark's "Splitting" House in Englewood, New Jersey from 1974, which seemed to allude to seismic changes ongoing in American familial life. At the time Matta-Clark stated: "Buildings are fixed entities in the minds of most people. The notion of mutable space is taboo, especially in one's own house. People live in their space with a temerity that is frightening."[14] ■ A more puckish and less somber take on domestic architecture comes from Japanese designer Shigeru Ban and his Curtain Wall House of 1995. Here, the notion of inside and out, private and public, formal and informal is turned into a campy bit of architectural theater. Only a giant, retractable white curtain separates the living spaces from the teeming Tokyo neighborhood. The pristine and geometric glass curtain wall, so loved by the heroic designers such as

buildings created by our culture. Aaron Betsky identifies the Victorian Cult of Domesticity, beginning in the early 1840s, as the point at which the home was divided into private and public spheres, both designed by male architects, but both largely ruled over by women. Betsky sees "a history of separation, in which men assigned a separate space to women and then constructed an architecture of wood, stones, and justifications that formalized these separate realms."[18] ■ Clark sees the Cult of Domesticity as "a new attempt to use architecture to promote a series of reforms that centered on Christian family life as the basis of a new social order."[19] While previously American families had largely lived and slept in common areas, this new order sought "new rooms for specific functions." And despite the era's piety about family unity, in fact the architecture, allowing for example separate bedrooms for children, was "encourag[ing] a greater degree of individuality, albeit within specifically designated limits." Many homes were even isolating: "The ideal emphasized the organic unity of the family that would protect it against the dangers of the outside world; the reality seemed more to be a group of atomistic individuals who came together only on special occasions such as mealtimes." ■ Regardless of how space is conceived, rendered, perceived and used, Zevi points to the timeless vertical and horizontal axes that drive building design: "When following a horizontal line in instinctive mimicry, man feels a sense of the imminent, the rational, the intellectual. It is parallel to the earth on which man walks and accordingly accompanies his movement . . . The vertical line [is] symbol of the infinite, of ecstasy, of emotion [figure 9]. To follow it, man must halt and raise his eyes to heaven, leaving, for a time, his normal visual direction."[20] ■ One of the most compelling examples of the procession of vertical/horizontal architectural space is Steven Holl's Simmons Hall dormitory at MIT [pages 12 right, 13, 15, 28-31, and 138-139]. The building is set on a long, narrow site at the southern edge of the campus. The exterior windows form a grid system that is color coded to gravitational stresses on the façade, a nod to the school's *über*-geek culture. Beginning at the lobby on a meandering, poured-in-place concrete ramp, occupants move slowly up and through a series of spaces [figure 10]. Views to the exterior are mixed with glimpses of common study and computer areas. The building's severely geometric exterior gives little hint of the freeform community spaces that Holl has positioned throughout the building, to be encountered almost spontaneously. Once in these rooms, the eye is drawn upward to skylights whose luminosity plays off of the curvilinear wall surfaces [figure 11], which are in

Notes

1. Siegfried Giedion, *Space, Time and Architecture* (Cambridge, MA: Harvard University Press, 1947), 515. ■ 2. Bruno Zevi, *Architecture as Space* (New York: Horizon Press, 1957), 22. ■ 3. Katherine F. Benzel, *The Room in Context: Design Beyond Boundaries* (New York: McGraw-Hill, 1997), 14. ■ 4. Benzel, 188. ■ 5. Zevi, 141. ■ 6. Franz Schulze, *Mies van der Rohe: A Critical Biography* (Chicago: University of Chicago Press, 1985), 146. ■ 7. Charles A. Riley II, *The Saints of Modern Art: The Ascetic Ideal in Contemporary Painting, Sculpture, Architecture, Music, Dance, Literature and Philosophy* (Hanover and London: University Press of New England, 1998), 169. ■ 8. Andres Janser, "Only Film Can Make the New Architecture Intelligible!" in *Cinema & Architecture*, François Penz and Maureen Thomas eds. (London, British Film Institute, 1997), 34. ■ 9. William J. Mitchell, *City Bits: Space, Place and the Infobahn* (Cambridge, MA: MIT Press, 1995), 101. ■ 10. Mitchell, 99. ■ 11. Quoted in *Architectural Review*, July 2003, 40. ■ 12. Carel Blotkamp, *Mondrian: The Art of Destruction* (New York: Harry Abrams, 1995), 148. ■ 13. Quoted in *Interior Design*, April 2003, 72. ■ 14. Quoted in Bill Arnung, "Arguing with Walls" in *Inside Space: Experiments in Redefining Rooms*, Joel Sanders, ed. (Cambridge, MA: MIT List Visual Arts Center, 2001), 30. ■ 15. Arnung, 34. ■ 16. Aaron Betsky, *Building Sex: Men, Women, Architecture, and the Construction of Sexuality* (New York: William Morrow and Company, 1995), xiv. ■ 17. L.K. Weisman, "Women's Environmental Rights: A Manifesto"

9
10

a gray material with the look and feel of the skin of a porpoise. At key points, entire sections are carved out of the building to accommodate open-air terraces and a "stoop" that overlooks the adjacent playing field. For this house of communal living and learning, Holl has succeeded in a fresh take on some old ideas about procession and spatial design. ■ The compelling work by Holl and other givers of spatial form is reciprocated in a sense by the users of their buildings. The experience of space requires a certain experiential rigor, an act of ownership, as described by Gaston Bachelard: ". . . every angle in a room, every inch of secluded space in which we like to hide, or withdraw into ourselves, is a symbol of solitude for the imagination; that is to say, it is the germ of a room . . . Consciousness of being at peace in one's corner produces a sense of immobility, and this, in turn, radiates immobility. An imaginary room rises up around our bodies . . . so we have to designate the space of our immobility by making it the space of our being. In *l'Etat d'Ebauche*, Nöel Arnaud writes: *'Je suis l'espace ou je suis.'* (I am the space where I am.)."[21]

in *Gender Space Architecture: An Interdisciplinary Introduction*, Rendell, Penner and Borden eds. (London and New York: Routledge, 2000), 1. ■ 18. Betsky, xiv. ■ 19. Robert Blair St. George (ed.), *Material Life in America, 1600-1860* (Boston: Northeastern University Press, 1988), 544. ■ 20. Zevi, 188. ■ 21. Gaston Bachelard, *The Poetics of Space* (Boston: Beacon Press, 1994), 177.

Image Captions

Figure 1: Ludwig Mies van der Rohe and Philip Johnson, Seagram Building, New York, 1958. ■ Figure 2: Frank Lloyd Wright, Guggenheim Museum, New York, 1959. ■ Figures 3–4: Zaha Hadid, Contemporary Arts Center, Cincinnati, 2003. ■ Figures 5–6: Weiss/Manfredi Architects, Museum of the Earth, Ithaca, New York, 2003. ■ Figures 7–8: Peter L. Gluck and Partners, Fowler Residence, New Canaan, Connecticut, 2002. ■ Figure 9: Steven Holl Architects, Chapel of St. Ignatius, Seattle, 1997. ■ Figures 10–11: Steven Holl Architects, Simmons Hall MIT, 2002.

entry

No part of a building is so suffused with ritual as the entry. ■ In Ancient Greek temples, the *pronaos* was an anteroom where worshippers prepared before entering and paying homage to the god. ■ In Roman villas and later in Renaissance Florentine palaces, a modest entry *fauces* opened on to a grand central courtyard. ■ Today architects manipulate entries for maximum effect. ■ Poet Robert Duncan Edwards wrote: "Here, in the foyer of my age, the passing of the storm remains upon the page where I reread myself, and all that once befell comes once again to fall. It is a text of after-images."

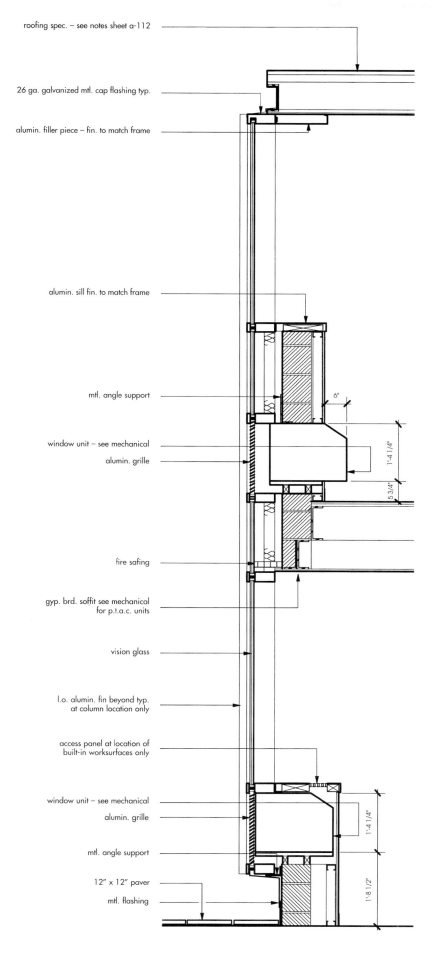

roofing spec. – see notes sheet a-112

26 ga. galvanized mtl. cap flashing typ.

alumin. filler piece – fin. to match frame

alumin. sill fin. to match frame

mtl. angle support

6"

window unit – see mechanical

alumin. grille

1'-4 1/4"

5 3/4"

fire safing

gyp. brd. soffit see mechanical for p.t.a.c. units

vision glass

l.o. alumin. fin beyond typ. at column location only

access panel at location of built-in worksurfaces only

window unit – see mechanical

alumin. grille

1'-4 1/4"

mtl. angle support

12" x 12" paver

mtl. flashing

1'-8 1/2"

Previous spread: Steven Holl Architects, Simmons Hall MIT, Cambridge, Massachusetts, 2003. This spread: Gary Shoemaker Architects, Transitional Services Inc., Queens, New York, 2000. This overtly modernist "glass box" is subsumed five feet below street level. The architect used this "moat" as an entry opportunity, forming a bridge and further identifying the entrance by a sleek, brushed metal canopy and a bright yellow plane, which forms a primary color counterpoint to the red cylinder that penetrates the building's ceiling.

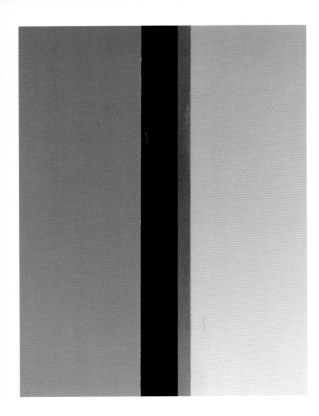

Bohlin Cywinski Jackson, Apple Store Tokyo, 2003. The stainless steel panels are attached to the wall system such that they appear to hover unsupported. The *sans serif* lettering over the entrance is engraved into the steel, lending dignity and elegance to the building entry.

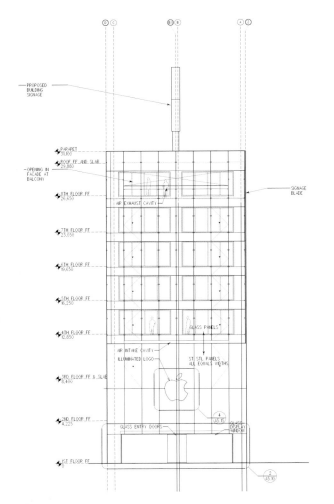

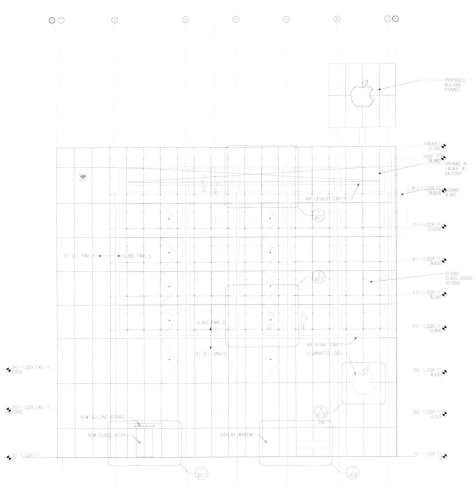

east and south elevations

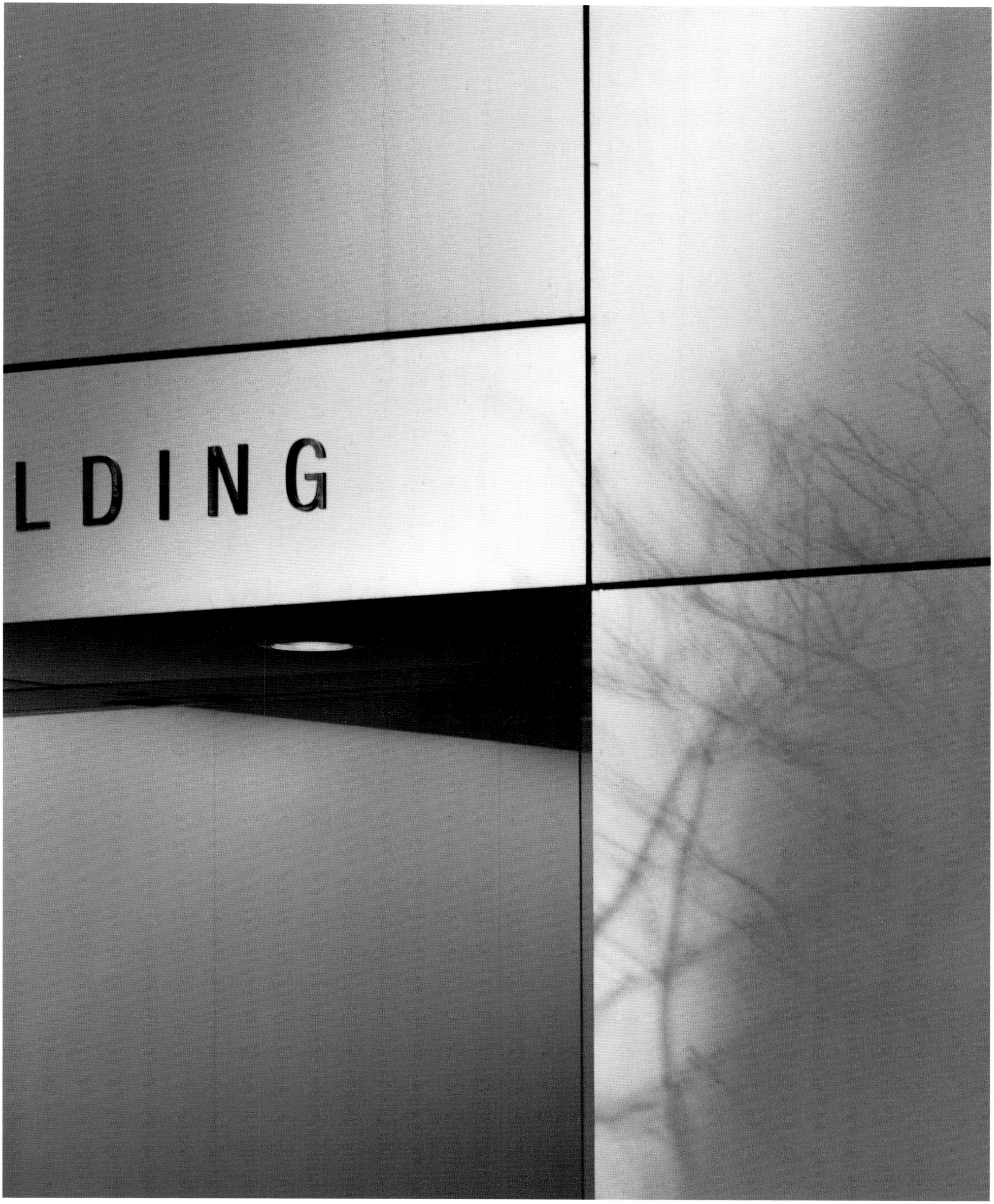
LDING

Peter L. Gluck and Partners, Little Sisters of the Assumption Family Health Services, New York, 2003. On this storefront façade, the rigid orthoganol geometry is broken only by the gray zinc siding in a gentle waving pattern and the slight angled ascent of the entrance ramp. Sunshades are formed over the windows and entry by extruded canopies.

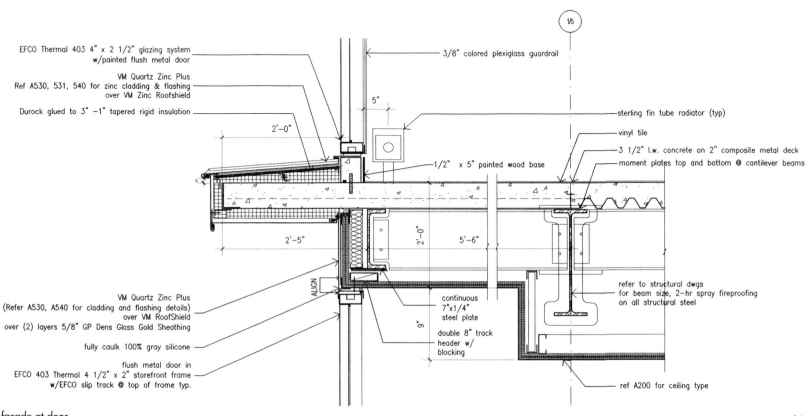

EFCO Thermal 403 4" x 2 1/2" glazing system w/painted flush metal door

VM Quartz Zinc Plus Ref A530, 531, 540 for zinc cladding & flashing over VM Zinc Roofshield

Durock glued to 3" −1" tapered rigid insulation

3/8" colored plexiglass guardrail

sterling fin tube radiator (typ)

vinyl tile

3 1/2" l.w. concrete on 2" composite metal deck

moment plates top and bottom @ cantilever beams

1/2" x 5" painted wood base

refer to structural dwgs for beam size, 2-hr spray fireproofing on all structural steel

VM Quartz Zinc Plus (Refer A530, A540 for cladding and flashing details) over VM RoofShield over (2) layers 5/8" GP Dens Glass Gold Sheathing

fully caulk 100% gray silicone

flush metal door in EFCO 403 Thermal 4 1/2" x 2" storefront frame w/EFCO slip track @ top of frame typ.

continuous 7"x1/4" steel plate

double 8" track header w/ blocking

ref A200 for ceiling type

façade at door

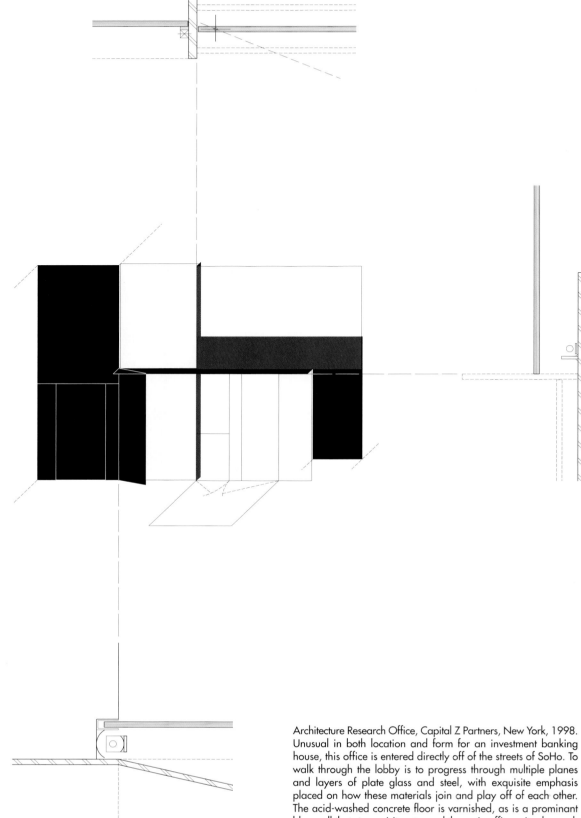

Architecture Research Office, Capital Z Partners, New York, 1998. Unusual in both location and form for an investment banking house, this office is entered directly off of the streets of SoHo. To walk through the lobby is to progress through multiple planes and layers of plate glass and steel, with exquisite emphasis placed on how these materials join and play off of each other. The acid-washed concrete floor is varnished, as is a prominant blue wall that steers visitors toward the main office suites beyond.

Steven Holl Architects, Makuhari Housing, Chiba, Japan, 1996. Holl conceived the entire complex as divided between "active, lightweight" and "silent, heavy" buildings. This stair forms the entry to an "active" building raised on pilotis.

Steven Holl Architects, University of Minnesota College of Architecture and Landscape Architecture, 2003. Clad in copper panels and channel glass, this entrance is a notch carved out of the cubic form and is marked by a canopy with a single support. At night, the channel glass façade glows like a welcoming beacon.

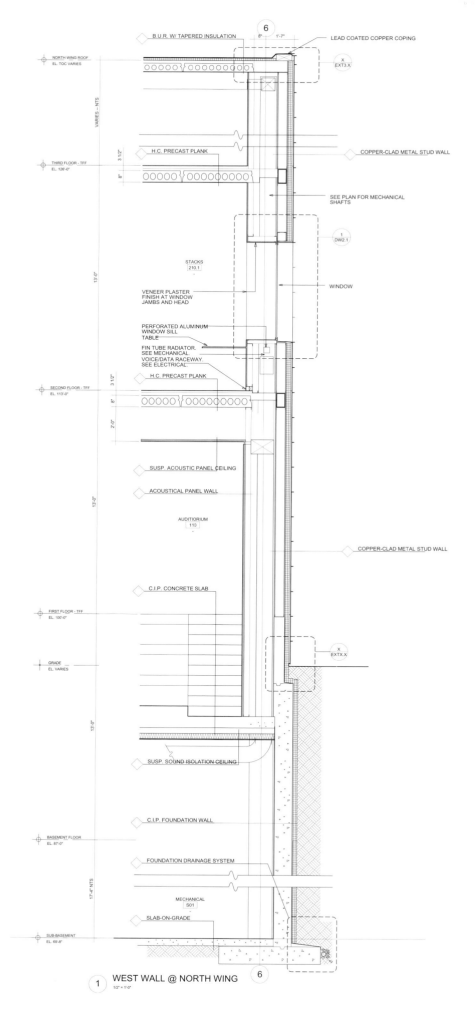

B.U.R. W/ TAPERED INSULATION

LEAD COATED COPPER COPING

NORTH WING ROOF
EL. TOC VARIES

COPPER-CLAD METAL STUD WALL

H.C. PRECAST PLANK

THIRD FLOOR - TFF
EL. 126'-0"

SEE PLAN FOR MECHANICAL SHAFTS

STACKS
210.1

WINDOW

VENEER PLASTER FINISH AT WINDOW JAMBS AND HEAD

PERFORATED ALUMINUM WINDOW SILL TABLE

FIN TUBE RADIATOR. SEE MECHANICAL. VOICE/DATA RACEWAY. SEE ELECTRICAL.

H.C. PRECAST PLANK

SECOND FLOOR - TFF
EL. 113'-0"

SUSP. ACOUSTIC PANEL CEILING

ACOUSTICAL PANEL WALL

AUDITIORIUM
110

COPPER-CLAD METAL STUD WALL

C.I.P. CONCRETE SLAB

FIRST FLOOR - TFF
EL. 100'-0"

GRADE
EL. VARIES

SUSP. SOUND ISOLATION CEILING

C.I.P. FOUNDATION WALL

BASEMENT FLOOR
EL. 87'-0"

FOUNDATION DRAINAGE SYSTEM

MECHANICAL
S01

SLAB-ON-GRADE

SUB-BASEMENT
EL. 69'-8"

1 WEST WALL @ NORTH WING
1/2" = 1'-0"

This and following spread: Steven Holl Architects, Simmons Hall MIT, Cambridge, Massachusetts, 2003. The building is long and narrow, and contains an entrance at its far eastern side closest to the rest of the campus. But this ceremonial entry is carved out of the center of the building's main façade. The steps face an athletic field and can double as informal viewing stands. A glass vitrine-like structure spans this entrance niche, and connects to the building's main circulation arteries.

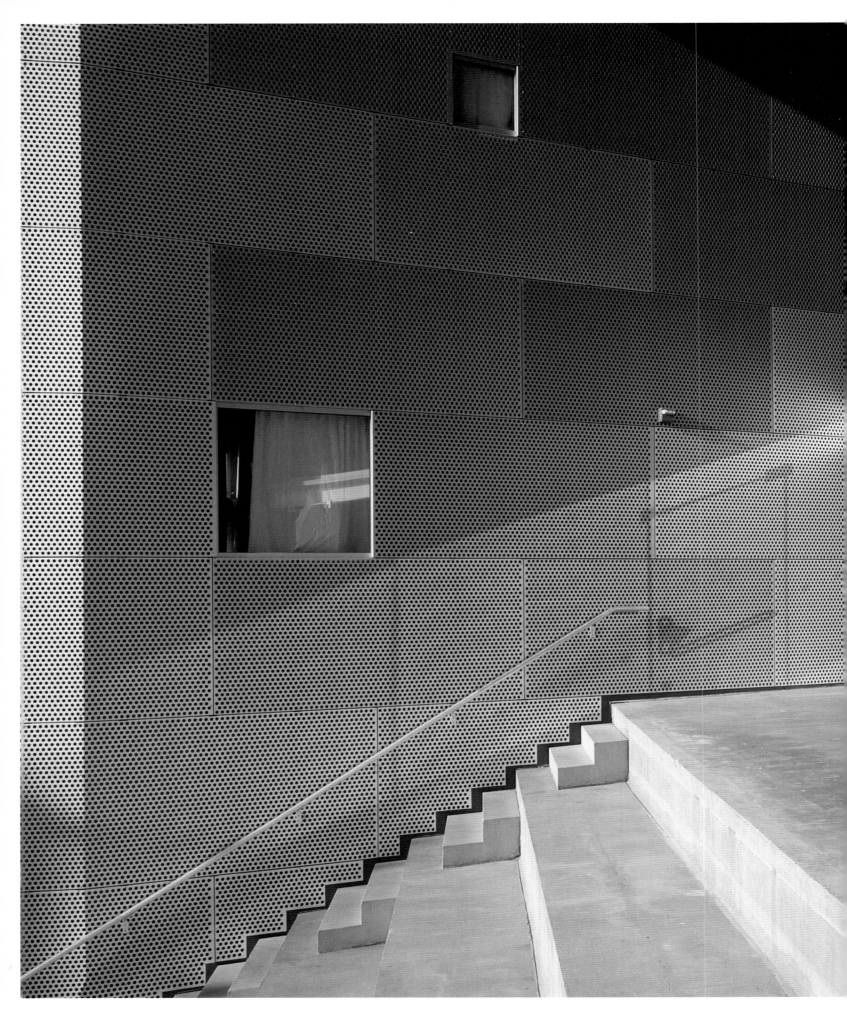

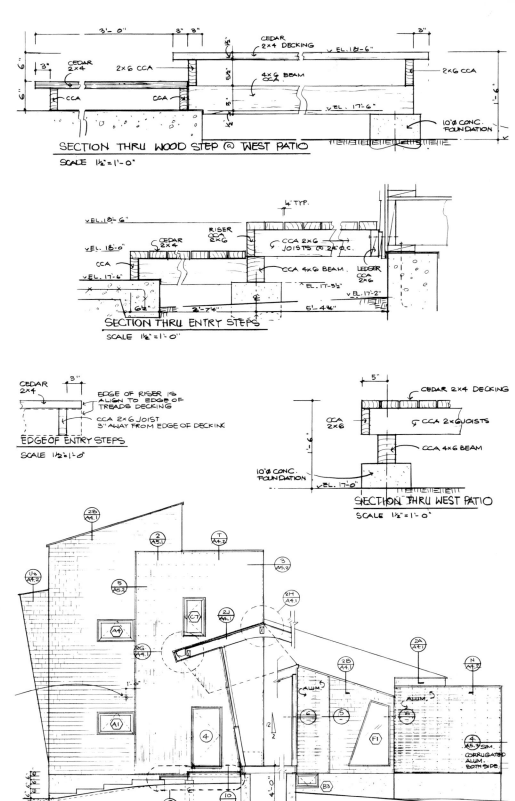

SECTION THRU WOOD STEP @ WEST PATIO
SCALE 1½" = 1'-0"

SECTION THRU ENTRY STEPS
SCALE 1½" = 1'-0"

EDGE OF ENTRY STEPS
SCALE 1½" = 1'-0"

SECTION THRU WEST PATIO
SCALE 1½" = 1'-0"

WEST ELEVATION - 2
SCALE ¼" = 1'-0"

Studio A/B, Hideaki Arizumi, Glynis M. Berry Architects, Architects' Weekend Home, Orient, New York, 1996. The house's design is formed by a series of interlocking volumes sheathed, alternately, in aluminum siding and cedar shingles. At the back entry these volumes meet, the cedar shingle wall having a slight cant and forming a welcoming overhang. Beyond the door, the floor-to-ceiling birch panelling provides both a warm enclosure and the convenience of built-in cabinetry for storage.

hallway

The hallway is the artery of a building. ■ "I hear doors shutting, countless doors down an endless hallway, endings that were once beginnings," wrote Michael S. Weaver. ■ Through hallways flow people who make a structure live. ■ It is about connection, anticipation, the excitement of what exists around the next corner or beyond the next door. ■ Designers must make these corridors efficient, but also appreciate their ritual importance. ■ Richard Shelton: "Dim lights will be on in the hallway, a long moss carpet flowing past a wilderness of doors, stairs crowded with unpredictable lovers and assassins."

Previous spread: Toshiko Mori Architect, Compound on the Gulf of Mexico, Sarasota, Florida, 2002. This spread: Bohlin Cywinski Jackson, The Keystone Building, Harrisburg, Pennsylvania, 2000. Exposed I-beams penetrate structural columns sheathed in granite. A wide lobby stairway forms a processional space organized by freestanding railings. Seen from the side, *enfilade* openings lend an added atmosphere of order and formality.

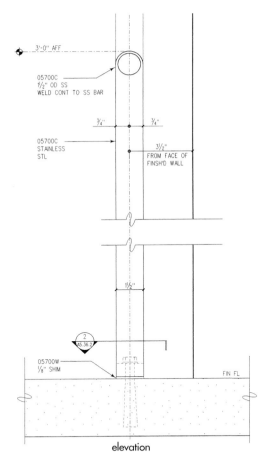

elevation   section

rail @ atrium plaza level   scale: 6″ = 1′-0″

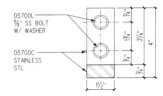

plans   scale: 6″ = 1′-0″

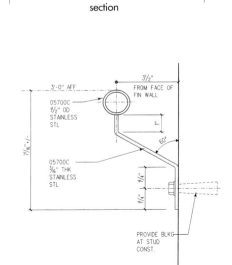

bracket section @ handrails

MAP Architecture + Design, Fallon New York, 2000. The elevator lobby for this advertising agency space picks up on the verticality of its location, Cass Gilbert's Woolworth Building, with white-washed maple struts set against backlit acrylic. A corridor that cuts perpendicular through the entrance hall is punctuated by a dramatic black cabinet in which are displayed constantly changing advertising samples, like museum pieces in transparent, lit vitrines.

Gabellini Associates, Jil Sander Showroom, Hamburg, 1997. A hallway leading to a stair has alcoves with recessed lighting, lending a sense of quiet drama. The asymmetrical stair contrasts with the enfilade-like series of wall recesses.

This and previous spread: Zaha Hadid Architects, Rosenthal Center for Contemporary Art, Cincinnati, 2003. Abandoning the notion of circulation corridors as neutral white cubes, the architect sees the variously shaped polygons and non-orthogonal angles as deliberate attempts to provoke and challenge the museum patron. Here, walls come together such to recall early supremacist compositions.

Steven Holl Architects, Texas Stretto House, Dallas, 1992. Holl's concept of this residence, located adjacent to a dam, is as a "spatial dam" with "aqueous space" flowing through it. Because the house is several wings set into a somewhat hilly site, different floor levels are required. In this central hallway, terrazzo floors step down to black concrete floors, while above the curving roof planes meet and intersect.

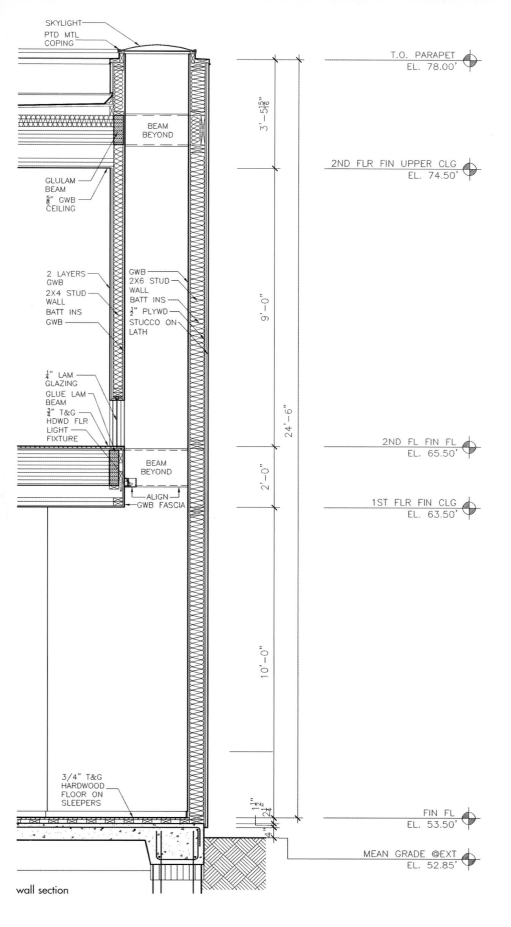

wall section

SKYLIGHT
PTD MTL COPING

T.O. PARAPET
EL. 78.00'

3'-5 15/16"

BEAM BEYOND

2ND FLR FIN UPPER CLG
EL. 74.50'

GLULAM BEAM
5/8" GWB CEILING

GWB
2X6 STUD WALL
BATT INS
1/2" PLYWD
STUCCO ON LATH

2 LAYERS GWB
2X4 STUD WALL
BATT INS
GWB

9'-0"

24'-6"

1/4" LAM GLAZING
GLUE LAM BEAM
3/4" T&G HDWD FLR
LIGHT FIXTURE

2ND FL FIN FL
EL. 65.50'

BEAM BEYOND

2'-0"

ALIGN
GWB FASCIA

1ST FLR FIN CLG
EL. 63.50'

10'-0"

3/4" T&G HARDWOOD FLOOR ON SLEEPERS

1 1/2"
2 1/4"
4"

FIN FL
EL. 53.50'

MEAN GRADE @EXT
EL. 52.85'

François de Menil, Architect, Bank Street Residence, Houston, 2000. Art as an organizing element: A provocative sculpture by Yves Klein is placed at a crucial nexus, underneath the stairway and at the end of the corridor, helping give the space a further sense of calm and order. In the stairwell, light streams in through both vertical window and skylight, while a horizontal ribbon window brings light into the adjoining bedroom.

Toshiko Mori Architect, House on the Gulf of Mexico, Sarasota, Florida, 2002. A stairway enclosed in glass rises directly from the ground level into a central atrium that is skylit by glass panels that subtly change color.

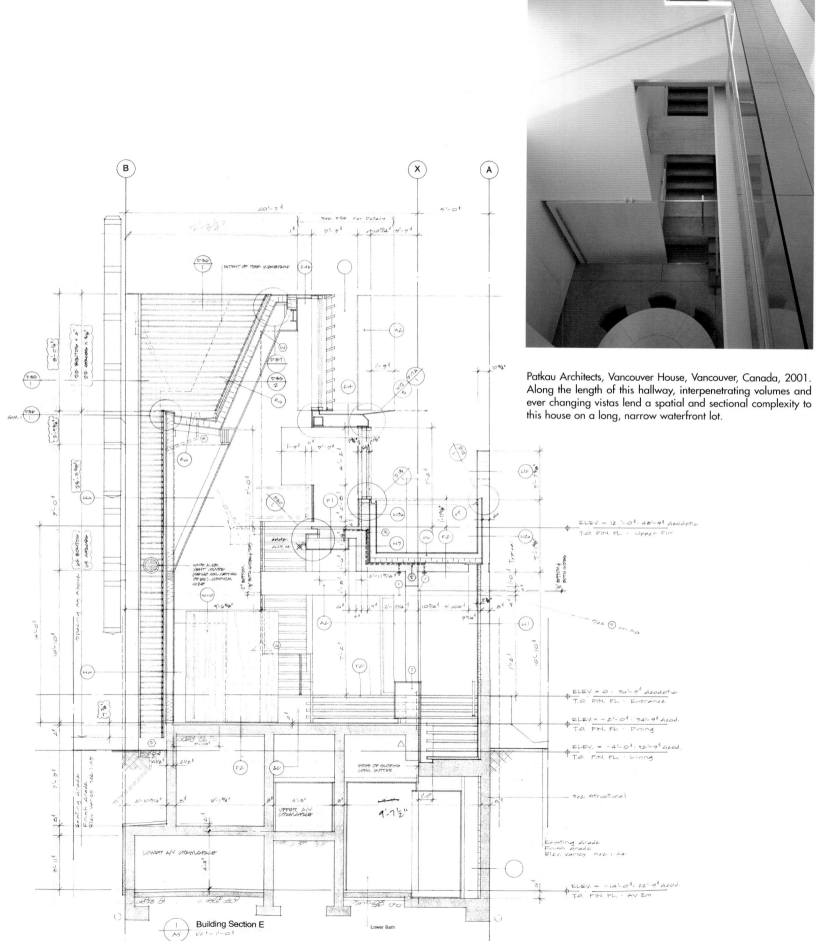

Building Section E

Lower Bath

Patkau Architects, Vancouver House, Vancouver, Canada, 2001.
Along the length of this hallway, interpenetrating volumes and
ever changing vistas lend a spatial and sectional complexity to
this house on a long, narrow waterfront lot.

ELEV = 12'-0", 48'-9" GEODETIC
T.O. FIN. FL · Upper Fl.

ELEV = 0', 36'-9" GEODETIC
T.O. FIN. FL · Entrance

ELEV = -2'-0", 34'-9" Geod.
T.O. FIN. FL · Dining

ELEV = -4'-0", 32'-9" Geod.
T.O. FIN. FL · Living

ELEV = -14'-0", 22'-9" Geod.
T.O. FIN. FL · AV Rm.

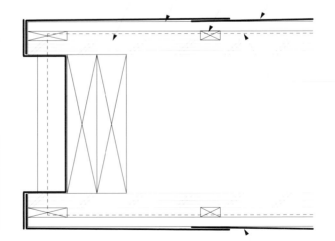

30 lb. felt on 3/4" plywood

1/2" presure treated horizontal sleepers wrapped in 30 lb. felt

1/2" presure treated horizontal sleepers wrapped in 30 lb. felt
18 gauge weathering steel shingles; painted on rear face as per specifications; fastened to sleeper system with 2" overlap to conceal stainless steel fasteners

dash line of concrete below

Architecture Research Office, Colorado House, 2000. A walk down the hallways becomes the unveiling of a series of mountain vistas. This house was essentially designed from the inside out, with the siting of all rooms and the positioning of all windows meant to provide the most spectacular views. The mullions of the large picture windows are in a pattern derived from the Golden Mean.

18 gauge stainless steel shingles

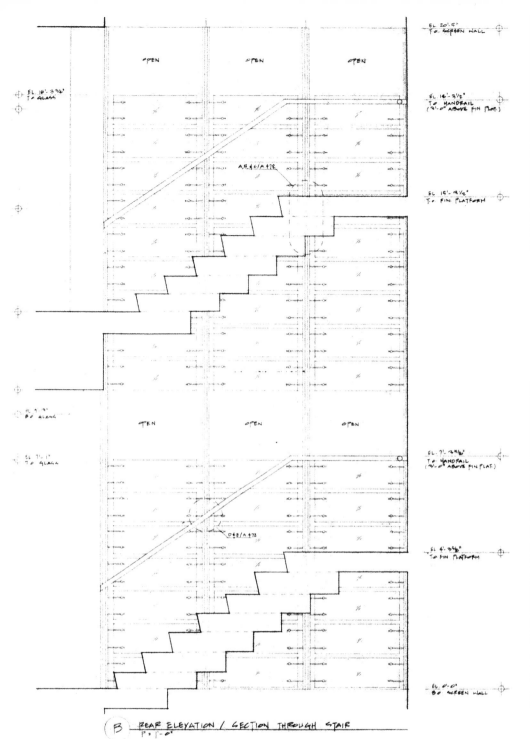

EL 20'-5"
T.O. SCREEN WALL

OPEN   OPEN   OPEN

EL 16'-3¾"
T.O. GLASS

EL 16'-3½"
TO HANDRAIL
(3'-0" ABOVE FIN PLAT.)

A, B, & C/A 478

EL 15'-3½"
T.O. FIN PLATFORM

EL 9'-9"
B.O. GLASS

OPEN   OPEN   OPEN

EL 7'-1"
T.O. GLASS

EL 7'-3⅝"
T.O. HANDRAIL
(3'-0" ABOVE FIN PLAT.)

D & B/A 478

EL 4'-3½"
T.O. FIN PLATFORM

EL 0'-0"
B.O. SCREEN WALL

B REAR ELEVATION / SECTION THROUGH STAIR
   1" = 1'-0"

Peter L. Gluck and Partners, Urban House, Brooklyn, New York, 1998. For this family, strict separation of semi-"public" and strictly private parts of the house was very important. Therefore, in this central skylit hallway, a screen of wood and glass partially hides the staircase. Another layer is added by doors that slide along tracks to close off the area completely. A Danish modern bench lends a quiet sense of order to the scheme.

Gwathmey-Siegel and Associates, Steel Loft, New York, 2001. The space's original structural columns are treated as the central organizing and aesthetic element, not unlike an ancient Greek or Roman colonnade. The spare white walls of this space are complemented by the lightness of the bleached maple floors. The 14 windows throw shards of light across this relatively blank architectural canvas.

great room

In the great room, with traditional living and dining rooms in a single open space, the egalitarian ideals of Modernism meet contemporary modes of living. ■ Often, these spaces feature varied ceiling heights and merge seamlessly into kitchens. ■ They accommodate entertaining and often find their focus on two elements: the table and the hearth. ■ Each speaks to notions about intimacy and sharing. Thomas Jefferson: "The bliss of the domestic fireside is the first boon of heaven." ■ M.F.K. Fisher: "Sharing food with another human being is an intimate act that should not be indulged in lightly."

Previous spread: Sam Trimble Architect, Roberts Apartment, New York, 2003. This spread: Hanrahan + Meyers Architects, Holley Loft, New York, 1993. A single crucial intervention completely redefines this open plan loft space: A wall of glass with precise black steel mullions that suggests the façade of a skyscraper. Suddenly the entire apartment becomes like the movie set of Alfred Hitchcock's paean to urban voyeurism, *Rear Window*. The great room can either be as open as a department store vitrine or closed off to sight and sound from the adjacent bedrooms with a large, thick curtain. Negotiating the border between the public and private, an interior space becomes a microcosm of the spatial dynamism of Manhattan life.

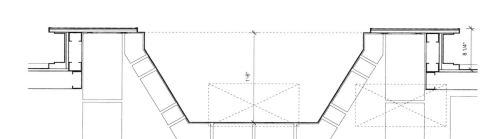

Shelton, Mindel & Associates, Mindel Loft, New York, 1997. A sun-washed rotunda is the central space of this expansive Greenwich Village home, leading to a living room that overlooks the cityscape. A simple white fireplace is flanked by matching twin windows; various seating arrangements throughout the room reflect a rich collection of mid-Century modernist furniture.

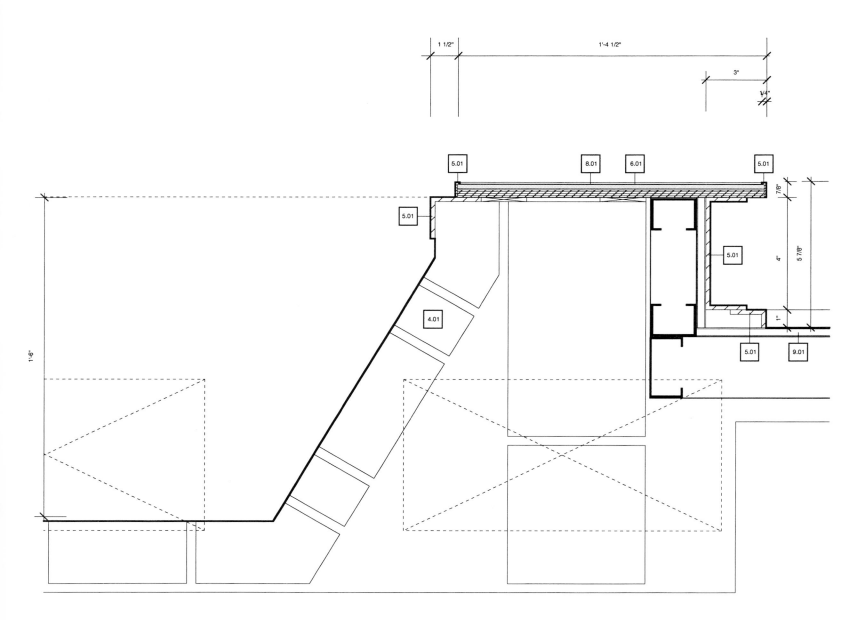

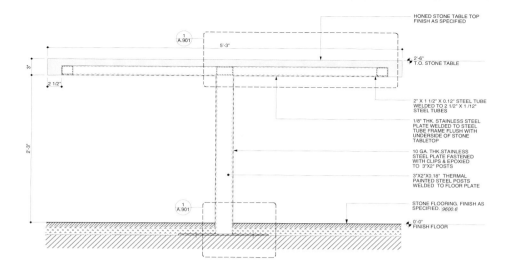

HONED STONE TABLE TOP
FINISH AS SPECIFIED

2'-6"
T.O. STONE TABLE

2" X 1 1/2" X 0.12" STEEL TUBE
WELDED TO 2 1/2" X 1 /12"
STEEL TUBES

1/8" THK. STAINLESS STEEL
PLATE WELDED TO STEEL
TUBE FRAME FLUSH WITH
UNDERSIDE OF STONE
TABLETOP

10 GA. THK.STAINLESS
STEEL PLATE FASTENED
WITH CLIPS & EPOXIED
TO 3"X2" POSTS

3"X2"X0.18" THERMAL
PAINTED STEEL POSTS
WELDED TO FLOOR PLATE

STONE FLOORING. FINISH AS
SPECIFIED. 9600.6

0'-0"
FINISH FLOOR

This and previous spread: Gabellini Associates, Olympic Tower
Residence, 2003. For this 49th floor aerie overlooking Midtown
Manhattan, an elemental purity of form and material frames
expansive views. Walls and floors in honed white Sivec marble
respond to the city's changing colors and textures throughout
daylight, twilight, and nightlight.

section and plan @ dining room stone table   scale 1-1 2"= 1'-0"

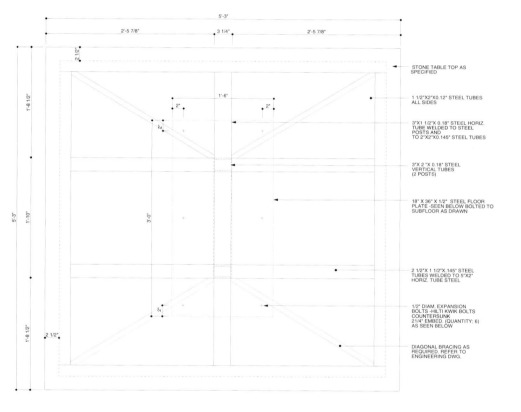

STONE TABLE TOP AS
SPECIFIED

1 1/2"X2"X0.12" STEEL TUBES
ALL SIDES

3"X1 1/2"X 0.18" STEEL HORIZ.
TUBE WELDED TO STEEL
POSTS AND
TO 2"X2"X0.145" STEEL TUBES

3"X 2 "X 0.18" STEEL
VERTICAL TUBES
(2 POSTS)

18" X 36" X 1/2" STEEL FLOOR
PLATE -SEEN BELOW BOLTED TO
SUBFLOOR AS DRAWN

2 1/2"X 1 1/2"X.145" STEEL
TUBES WELDED TO 5"X2"
HORIZ. TUBE STEEL

1/2" DIAM. EXPANSION
BOLTS -HILTI KWIK BOLTS
COUNTERSUNK
2 1/4" EMBED. (QUANTITY: 6)
AS SEEN BELOW

DIAGONAL BRACING AS
REQUIRED. REFER TO
ENGINEERING DWG.

Zoran with consulting Architects Peter Moore and Peter Pennoyer, Zoran Loft, New York, 1994. A former Greenwich Village industrial space is reinvented as minimalism at its most reductive extreme. Everything the least bit extraneous has been stripped away; newly plasered walls are covered in glossy white paint, while white epoxy floors seem to amplify the space by creating reflection upon reflection. There are no "rooms" to speak of, only a shallow stair leading to a sleeping area furnished with a futon. Dining takes place around a low table surrounded by cushions.

Diane Lewis Architect, Architect's Atelier, 1997. Like in some house interiors in Mediterranean islands, this space's even chromatics nonetheless reveal a rich range of textures, finishes and degrees of luminosity. Overall there is a sense of a primeval enclosure, sort of an urban archeological dig that reveals traces of the building's past while serving as a backdrop for a vibrant collection of architectural ephemera.

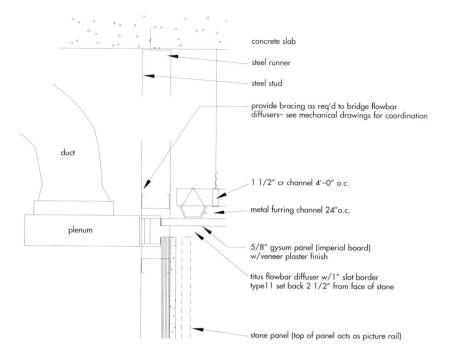

concrete slab

steel runner

steel stud

provide bracing as req'd to bridge flowbar
diffusers– see mechanical drawings for coordination

duct

1 1/2" cr channel 4'–0" o.c.

metal furring channel 24"o.c.

plenum

5/8" gysum panel (imperial board)
w/veneer plaster finish

titus flowbar diffuser w/1" slot border
type11 set back 2 1/2" from face of stone

stone panel (top of panel acts as picture rail)

ceiling detail

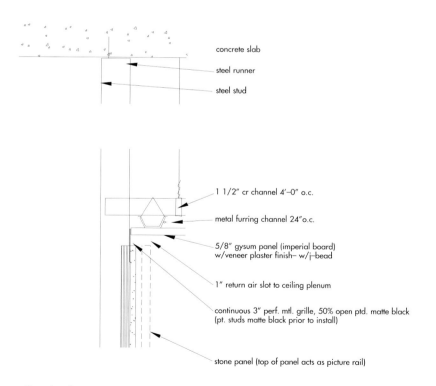

concrete slab

steel runner

steel stud

1 1/2" cr channel 4'–0" o.c.

metal furring channel 24"o.c.

5/8" gysum panel (imperial board)
w/veneer plaster finish– w/j–bead

1" return air slot to ceiling plenum

continuous 3" perf. mtl. grille, 50% open ptd. matte black
(pt. studs matte black prior to install)

stone panel (top of panel acts as picture rail)

ceiling detail

This, previous and following spread: Sam Trimble Architect, Roberts Apartment, New York, 2003. Mitered slabs of Portuguese limestone for walls form a chromatic mediation between darker brown furniture and slightly lighter floors and works of art. Responding to the client's desire to have a space that was "cave like," the architect chose materials that suggest geological permanence, their slight color variations juxtaposed against their rich variety of textures and surface reflectance.

Parsons + Fernandez-Casteleiro Architects PC, Fifth Avenue Apartment, New York, 1995. Created by combining adjacent units, this long, narrow space has windows at either end. The "day zone" great room is given the most window exposure, while the "night zone" of the flat is demarcated by a row of glass doors that allow in light and that pivot at their center points. A platform "loggia" at the end of the great room is slightly raised above floor level and leads to a small park-view terrace.

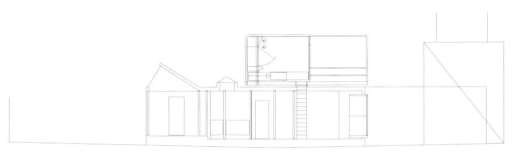

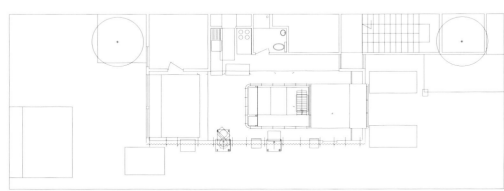

LOT/EK, Guzman Penthouse, New York, 1996. The longitudinal wall constitutes the visual and functional spine of this space, a living/dining/kitchen area formed out of a former mechanical room in a building adjacent to the Empire State Building. Above this great room, a bedroom is created out of a used shipping container. In the main space, refrigerator boxes are filled with technological functions: listen (hi-fi system), read (bookcase), and watch (video intercom, pull-out TV set and vertical monitor).

bedroom

The bedroom was not always so private—during the Middle Ages and the Renaissance, the royal bedchamber would often be filled with courtiers during a birth, to verify the legitimacy of the heir. ■ Today, bedrooms are generally considered the most intimate of spaces—part sanctuary, part repository of the most prized possessions. ■ Luxury hotels, seeking an edge, are challenged to offer opulence as well as attitude with rooms that satisfy the twin desires of comfort and *wanderlust*. ■ Edwin Muir: "Now in the bedroom where the pillows gleam, great and mysterious as deep hills of snow, an inaccessible land."

Previous spread: Calvin Klein, Model Bedroom for Advertisement, New York, 1998. This spread: Toshiko Mori Architect, Compound on the Gulf of Mexico, Sarasota, Florida, 2002. For this bedroom overlooking the gulf, poured concrete walls and overhang are matched with ribbon like windows that run the length of the upper façade.

This spread: François de Menil, Architect, Bank Street Residence, Houston, 2000. Only a freeform Frank Gehry chair breaks the otherwise angular shape of this room, lit both by a large picture window and a ribbon-shaped portal opening on the adjoining stairwell. A minimalist platform bed contrast with the effusive curved plywood chair. Following spread: Sam Trimble Architect, Roberts Apartment, New York, 2003. Indirect lighting highlights the texture of the bedroom's limestone walls, meant to evoke the safety and silence of a cave dwelling.

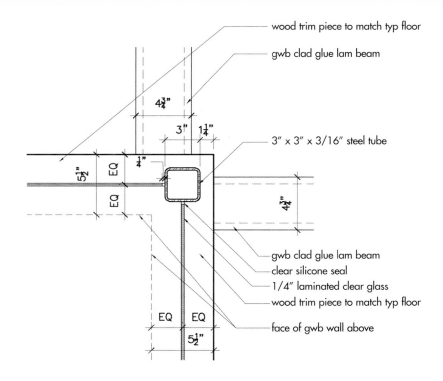

wood trim piece to match typ floor

gwb clad glue lam beam

3" x 3" x 3/16" steel tube

gwb clad glue lam beam
clear silicone seal
1/4" laminated clear glass
wood trim piece to match typ floor
face of gwb wall above

plan at interior corner glazing

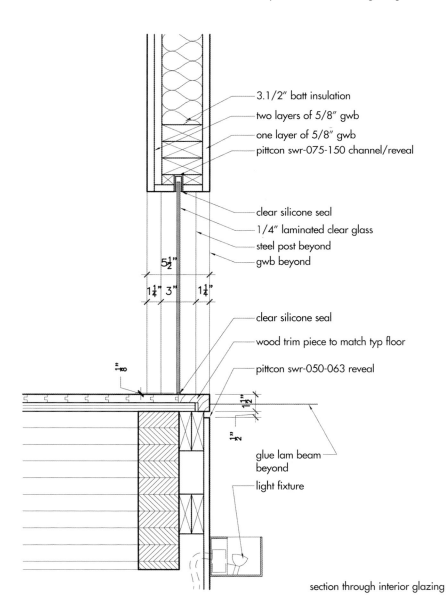

3.1/2" batt insulation
two layers of 5/8" gwb
one layer of 5/8" gwb
pittcon swr-075-150 channel/reveal

clear silicone seal
1/4" laminated clear glass
steel post beyond
gwb beyond

clear silicone seal
wood trim piece to match typ floor
pittcon swr-050-063 reveal

glue lam beam beyond

light fixture

section through interior glazing

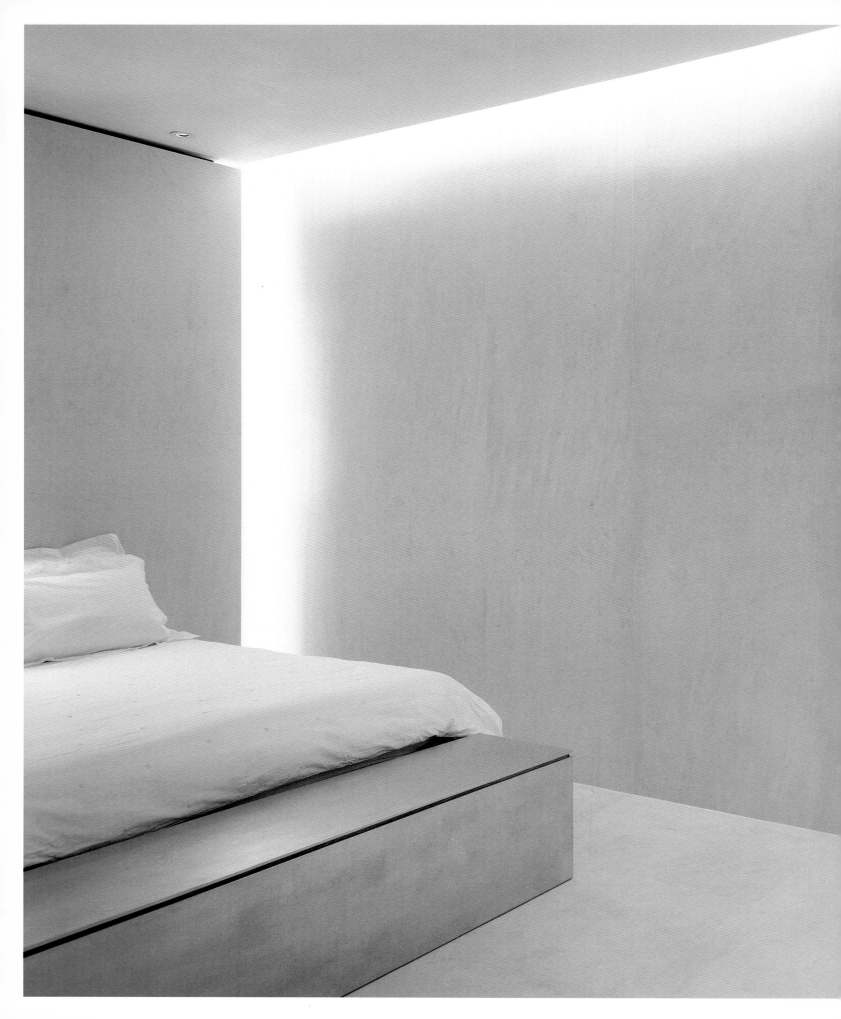

Michael Gabellini of Gabellini Associates in collaboration with Jay Smith, West 12th Street Residence, New York, 1989. "All rising to a great place is by a winding stair," said Francis Bacon. Here the sequence is reversed. In a duplex apartment, the stair, composed of slabs of white marble balanced on a central spine, leads directly to a bedroom below the main living area. At the far end, wall meets floor in a seamless platform meant to accommodate sparsely framed artwork.

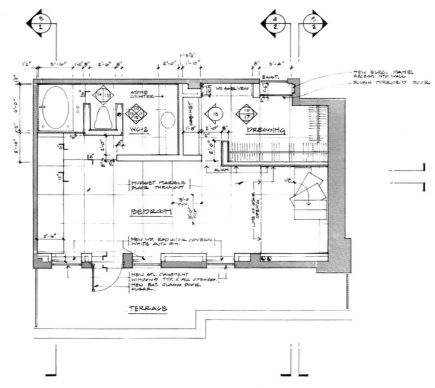

Studio MDA, West Village Townhouse, New York, 2003. The architectural detail of the ground floor of this townhouse was preserved and given a traditional color treatment. However, in this top floor master bedroom, the white wall/dark floor idea was reversed. The wall cabinetry is conceived as a continuous ribbon of dark stained mahogany, with the floors red oak stained white.

Resolution: 4 Architecture, TriBeCa Loft, 1997. This long and narrow former industrial space offered the opportunity to have each living area placed single file: entry, living, dining, kitchen then bedroom. New windows were punched at the extreme end to bring light into the master suite. So the rest of the space could benefit, sliding acrylic panels at once provide privacy while sharing light.

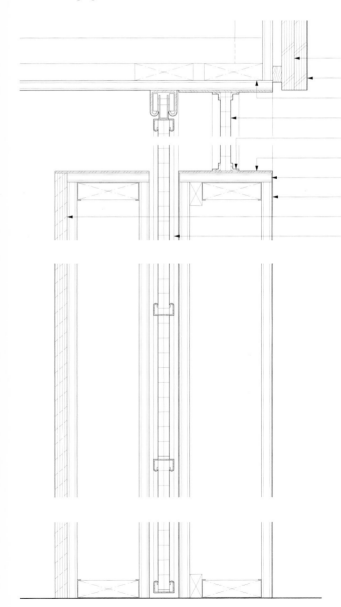

— 3/4" plywood

— 3/4" maple veneer plywood

— 2 x 4 wood blocking

— clear polygal panel

— 1/2" x 1/2" alum. angle

— 1/8" alum. flat stock

— 5/8" gwb

— stainless steel panel

— 3/4" mdf panel

— door & guide concealed between walls and mounted on floor

Arne Jacobsen, SAS House Room 606, Copenhagen, 1960. Like a time capsule of Jet Age design, this room is presented just as it was when the hotel opened. The Danish designer's trademark Swan and Egg chairs are in turquoise, as are the custom fabrics, matched with dark paneling and built-in cabinetry. The entire space feels like an ode to a more innocent time, when jet travel was carefree and exciting and airlines sought to capture the spirit of the times in everything from their logos to their silverware.

bathroom

It is in a bathroom where human beings come into the most intimate contact with building materials and textures. ■ Like kitchens, bathrooms were often a separate structure and did not become part of the contiguous house until early in the twentieth century. ■ Classic bathroom materials such as tile, marble and exposed plumbing fixtures can give the room the functional look so prized by early modernists. ■ From Eric Linklater's *Juan in America*: "There won't be any revolution in America . . . .The people are all too clean . . . .You can't feel fierce and revolutionary in a bathroom."

Previous spread: Gwathmey Siegel & Associates Architects, Residence in Police Building, New York, 2002. This spread: Gabellini Associates, Colleen Rosenblat Showroom, Hamburg, 1998. An alcove off of the showroom houses a small staff kitchen and a powder room, whose counter is a 1,200-pound slab of Sivec marble. The sink trap is concealed within this monolith. George Nakashima furniture provides casual seating.

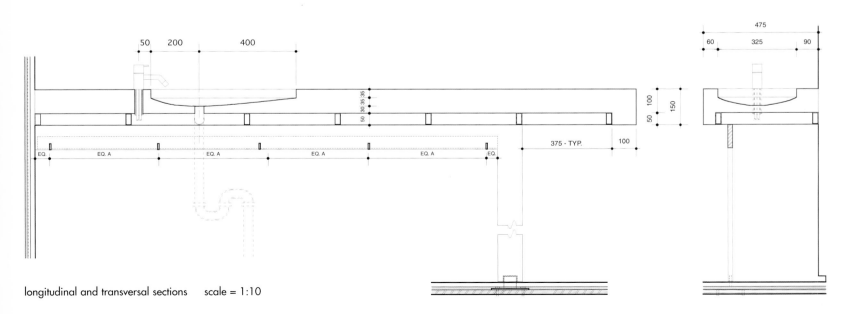

longitudinal and transversal sections   scale = 1:10

Michael Gabellini of Gabellini Associates in collaboration with Jay Smith, West 12th Street Residence, New York, 1989. A bath faced in white marble to match the apartment's stairway is separated from the bedroom with wide pane of ground glass.

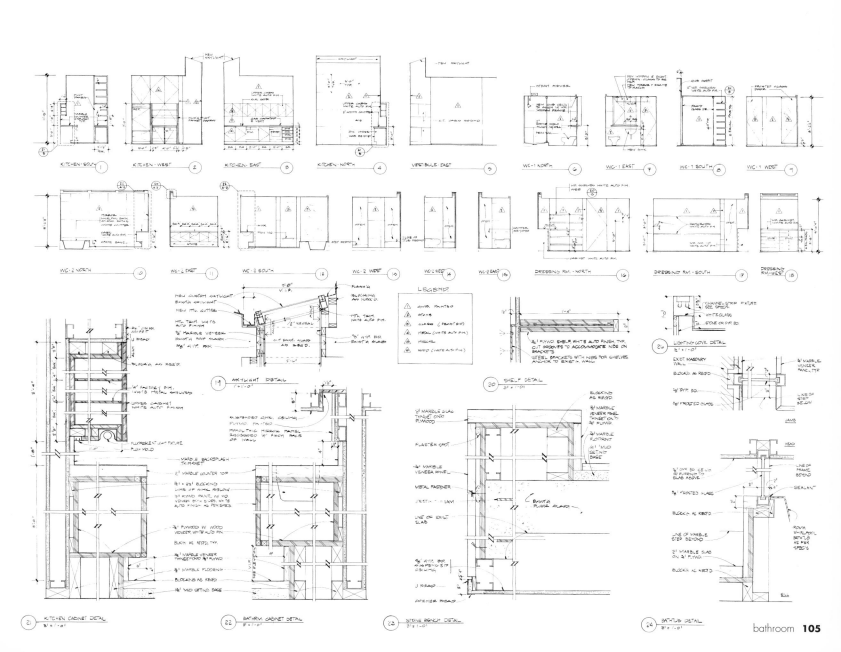

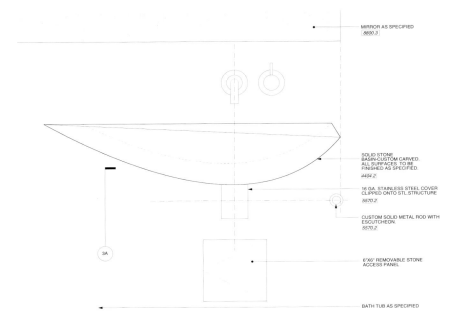

Gabellini Associates, Olympic Tower Residence, 2003. The bathroom in this Midtown apartment is separated from the bedroom only by a glass partition. Both the sink and tub are monolithic, carved blocks of white Sivec marble. The bathroom is raised on a stone plinth under which water drains through stone troughs, as in the baths of ancient Rome.

MIRROR AS SPECIFIED
8800.3

SOLID STONE
BASIN-CUSTOM CARVED.
ALL SURFACES TO BE
FINISHED AS SPECIFIED.
4404.2

16 GA. STAINLESS STEEL COVER
CLIPPED ONTO STL.STRUCTURE
5570.2

CUSTOM SOLID METAL ROD WITH
ESCUTCHEON.
5570.2

6"X6" REMOVABLE STONE
ACCESS PANEL

3A

BATH TUB AS SPECIFIED

elevation @ stone vanity @ master bath   scale 3"=1'-0"

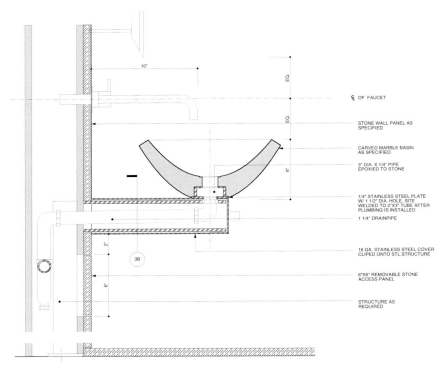

10"

EQ

EQ

℄ OF FAUCET

STONE WALL PANEL AS
SPECIFIED

CARVED MARBLE BASIN
AS SPECIFIED

3" DIA. X 1/4" PIPE
EPOXIED TO STONE

1/4" STAINLESS STEEL PLATE
W/ 1 1/2" DIA. HOLE. SITE
WELDED TO 2"X3" TUBE AFTER
PLUMBING IS INSTALLED

1 1/4" DRAINPIPE

16 GA. STAINLESS STEEL COVER
CLIPED ONTO STL.STRUCTURE

6"X6" REMOVABLE STONE
ACCESS PANEL

STRUCTURE AS
REQUIRED

3B

section @ stone vanity @ master bath   scale 3"=1'-0"

Sam Trimble Architect, Roberts Apartment, New York, 2003. This entire industrial space is sheathed in Portuguese lens limestone, in response to a client's desire for a cave like environment. The basin is a wide trough made of Purbeck Cap marble from Wales. Knobs and handles are dispensed with completely in favor of automatic sensor-controlled water flow, keyed from cold to hot across the cascade.

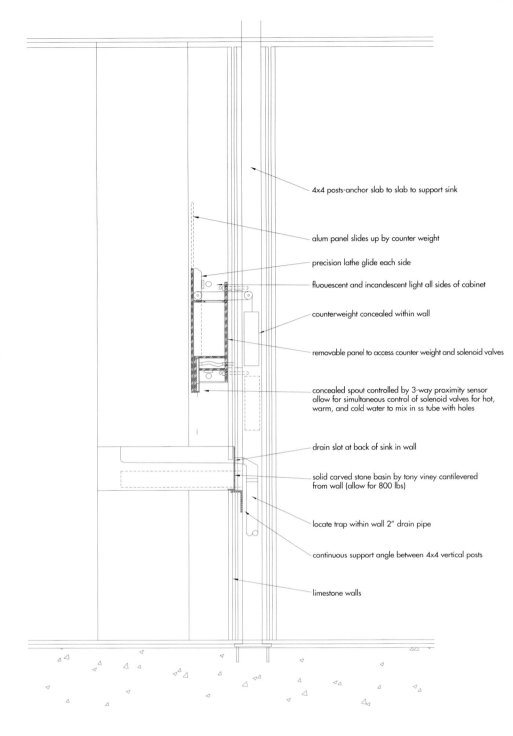

4x4 posts-anchor slab to slab to support sink

alum panel slides up by counter weight

precision lathe glide each side

fluouescent and incandescent light all sides of cabinet

counterweight concealed within wall

removable panel to access counter weight and solenoid valves

concealed spout controlled by 3-way proximity sensor allow for simultaneous control of solenoid valves for hot, warm, and cold water to mix in ss tube with holes

drain slot at back of sink in wall

solid carved stone basin by tony viney cantilevered from wall (allow for 800 lbs)

locate trap within wall 2" drain pipe

continuous support angle between 4x4 vertical posts

limestone walls

Sam Trimble Architect, Inc., Roberts Apartment, New York, 2003. Primeval cave dwelling meets luxurious spa. A waterfall splashing onto the bathroom's floor serves as the shower; in a corner, an azure pool is dappled with pebbles.

Studio MDA, West Village Townhouse, New York, 2003. The renovation of this landmark townhouse was conceived to preserve the ornate period detail of the lower floor while making each floor progressively more modern. This second-floor guest bathroom shows how the white wall/dark floor scheme of the first floor has been reversed, with dark stained mahogany cabinetry contrasting with the light floors.

Studio MDA, West Village Townhouse, New York, 2003. A shower area is formed by a precise cube of glass that faces a wall of dark-stained mahogany. Inside the shower is a minimalist composition of stainless steel controls, and the floor is a deeply-veined white marble.

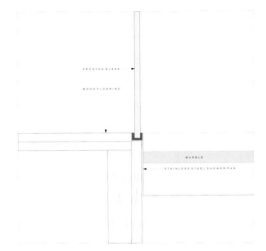

glass enclosure section detail

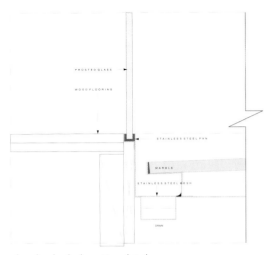

glass backsplash section detail

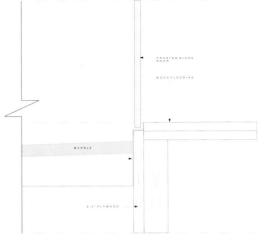

door section detail

Archi-Tectonics, Wooster Street Loft, New York, 1999. A metal and glass partition with an angled surface defines the bathroom in this loft space. The functional parts—the tub, sink and shower—are conceived as a single, continuous concrete element, with the mortar cast with blue pigment in wood forms. The industrial stainless steel toilet and surrounding paneling are normally used for prison cells.

Toshiko Mori Architect, Compound on the Gulf of Mexico, Sarasota, Florida, 2002. Both the sinks and bathtub are conceived as vessels somewhat detached from the rest of the room. Perforated metal panels form a machine like contrast to rough concrete and blue tile surfaces.

LeRoy Street Studio, Family Compound, Long Island, New York, 2003. A rich and multi-textured approach with dark wood and stone work. At a single point at the upper left wall, window, skylight and mirror all meet. For "his and hers" bathrooms, opaque glass covers most of the surfaces in the wife's version, while for him a more masculine attitude is assumed with surfaces covered in Portuguese azul ataij limestone.

Suyama Peterson Deguchi, Fauntleroy House, Seattle, 2003. The sink is built into an elegant alcove, while the tub is actually a sky-lit pool with water falling gently from a turret. Ceramics and stones add a calm Asian sensibility to this personal space.

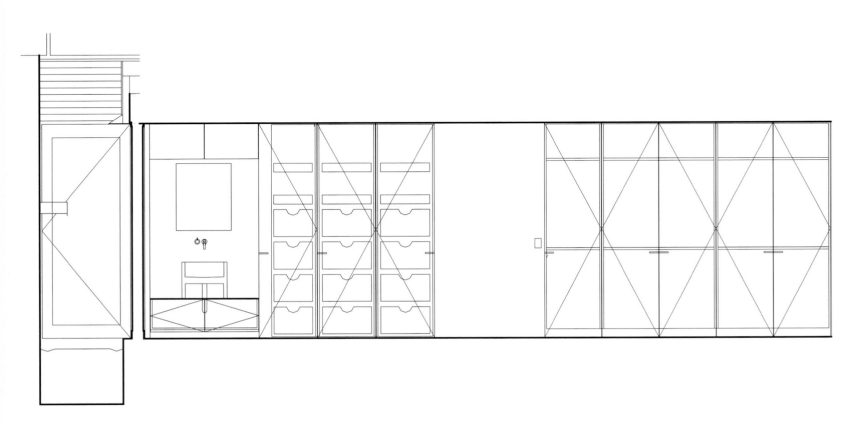

terrace

One of the goals of the master modernists was to blur, or even erase, what was perceived to be the arbitrary distinction between inside and out. ■ The terrace is a space that strides this boundary, offering both enclosure and exposure to nature. ■ Lord Alfred Tennyson: "Your triple terrace growing green and greener every May." ■ These outdoor rooms are as carefully designed and proportioned as any contained by walls. ■ Jorge Luis Borges: "In it and it alone do they exist, the gardens and the patios. The past retains them in that circular preserve which embraces dawn and dusk."

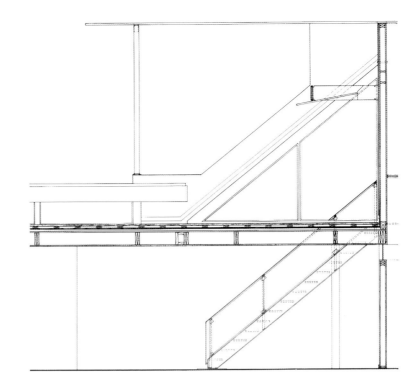

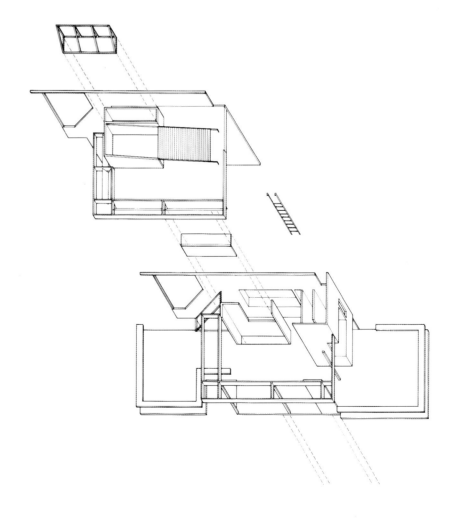

This and previous spread: Smith-Miller + Hawkinson, House for a Film Producer, Beverly Hills, 1999. This house on a compact hillside site, the great southern California modernist tradition, reads as a series of buildings connected by wood terraces. The original house was by a colleague of Richard Neutra, and a blurring of the inside/outside dichotomy is evident in this latest architectural intervention on the site.

Suyama Peterson Deguchi, Fauntleroy House, Seattle, 2003. A continuous stream engages the house along the northern edge, narrowing and then terminating in a pool. Alongside the water, the house's program unfolds in a syncopation of spaces. The deep overhanging eaves call to mind the work of Richard Neutra; the stucco walls and cascade of water suggests the best work of Luis Barragan.

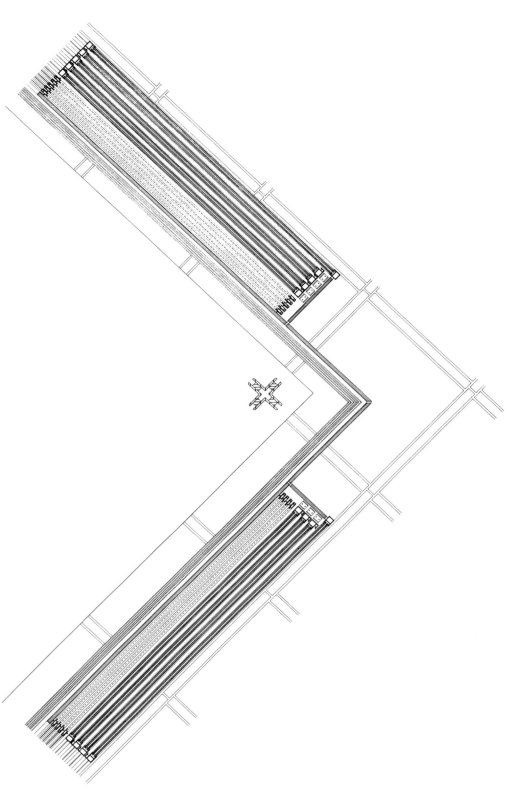

Peter L. Gluck and Partners, Architects, Addition to a 1955 Ludwig Mies van der Rohe Private Home, Weston, Connecticut, 1992. The existing house was classically Miesian, essentially an oblong glass and metal box. In order to make it more workable for the new owners, Gluck borrowed from other Mies buildings, especially the Barcelona Pavilion, by adding wings that feature wide overhanging eaves. This created numerous terraces around the perimeter of the new compound. "Walls" composed of exquisitely proportioned white steel grids help tie the disparate elements together. They are also suggestive of traditional Japanese interior screens, credited as inspirations to modernists like Mies.

Previous spread: LeRoy Street Studio, Family Compound, Long Island, New York, 2003. Recalling some of the best work of both Richard Neutra and Mies van der Rohe, this terrace space is shaded by a cantilevering roof overhang supported by a single column. This spread: François de Menil, Architect, Byzantine Fresco Chapel Museum, Houston, 1997. Conceived as a transitional space between the sanctuary and the chapel garden, this serene terrace is bounded by rough stone walls. Black Brazilian slate paving bridges a small moat fed by a fountain, which actually takes on the appearance of a primordial spring. A bench of ebonized cypress completes this place of respite and spiritual rejuvenation.

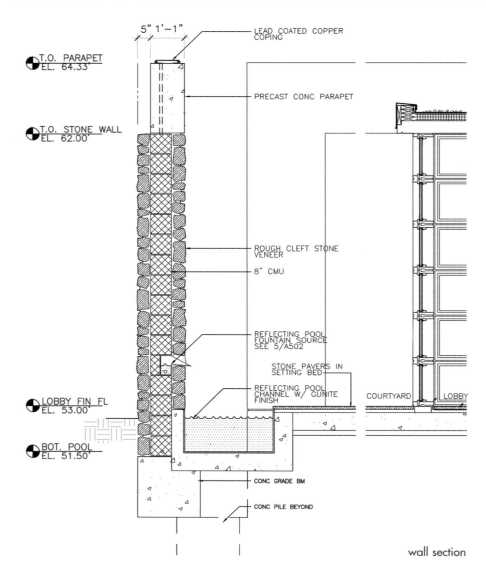

5" 1'-1"

T.O. PARAPET
EL. 64.33'

LEAD COATED COPPER COPING

PRECAST CONC PARAPET

T.O. STONE WALL
EL. 62.00'

ROUGH CLEFT STONE VENEER

8" CMU

REFLECTING POOL FOUNTAIN SOURCE SEE 5/A502

STONE PAVERS IN SETTING BED

REFLECTING POOL CHANNEL W/ GUNITE FINISH

COURTYARD   LOBBY

LOBBY FIN FL
EL. 53.00'

BOT. POOL
EL. 51.50'

CONC GRADE BM

CONC PILE BEYOND

wall section

Gabellini Associates, Ferragamo Store, New York, 2001. A central courtyard space allows the entire store to be viewed at once. A single platform built into the wall suggests an area for seating or display. In sales areas, floating plaster ceiling planes and suspended wall panels intensify the spirit of movement while directing the customer through the articulated spatial sequences.

Steven Holl Architects, Simmons Hall MIT, Cambridge, Massachusetts, 2003. Notches were cut at key points along the façade, forming terraces that overlook the playing fields that front along the building. The exterior grid system shows the numerous windows that are allowed for each room, and also act to minimize the exterior mass of the building.

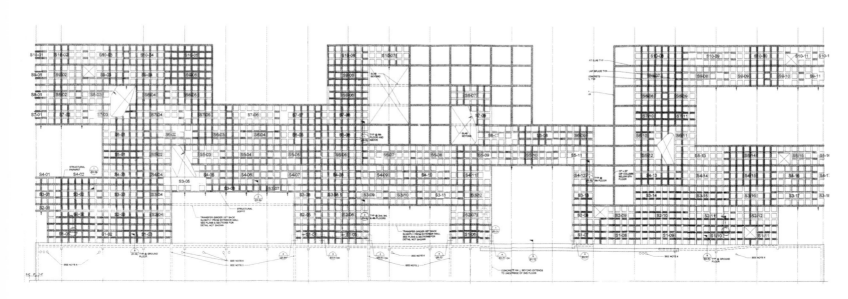

south elevation structural diagram

office

In the post–World War II era in the United States, modern architecture fused with corporate culture to create a powerful aesthetic. ■ Behind sleek glass curtain walls and amidst abstract art and brightly colored Knoll furniture, an image of cheerful efficiency held sway. ■ Now, an executive might as likely work out of a small office or even a cubicle. ■ And he or she will certainly have an office at home. ■ Just as the previous partitions between rooms gradually disappear, so does the dichotomy between work and residence. ■ The "study" has become a study in work efficiency.

Previous spread: Gerner Kronick Valcarcel Architects, M2L Showroom, New York, 2000. This and following spread: Gabellini Associates, Jil Sander Showroom, New York, 1996. This space is meant to replicate the simple and reductive designs of the Jil Sander collection. Polished concrete floors and white walls provide the quiet backdrop for dramatic Arne Jacobsen chairs in black leather. Indirect lighting in the space is provided in part by a wand fixture designed by Gabellini Associates that cantilevers out from a wall volume.

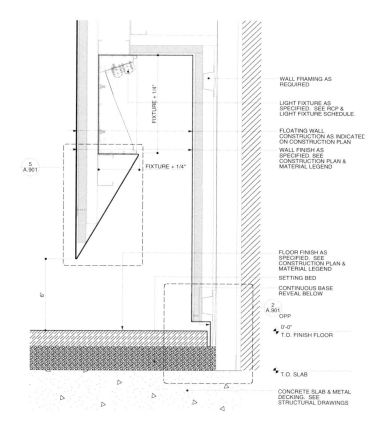

WALL FRAMING AS
REQUIRED

LIGHT FIXTURE AS
SPECIFIED. SEE RCP &
LIGHT FIXTURE SCHEDULE.

FLOATING WALL
CONSTRUCTION AS INDICATED
ON CONSTRUCTION PLAN

WALL FINISH AS
SPECIFIED. SEE
CONSTRUCTION PLAN &
MATERIAL LEGEND

FLOOR FINISH AS
SPECIFIED. SEE
CONSTRUCTION PLAN &
MATERIAL LEGEND

SETTING BED

CONTINUOUS BASE
REVEAL BELOW

OPP

0'-0"
T.O. FINISH FLOOR

T.O. SLAB

CONCRETE SLAB & METAL
DECKING. SEE
STRUCTURAL DRAWINGS

FIXTURE + 1/4"

FIXTURE + 1/4"

5
A.901

2
A.901

section detail @ floating fin wall   scale 3"=1'-0"

Helfand Architecture, Time Out New York Offices, New York, 1995. For the offices of a weekly magazine, the open space was designed along a single "street" with "neighborhoods" of clustered work stations along the way. Open duct work, exposed wiring and inexpensive off-the-shelf materials helped keep the project on a very low budget while retaining an open loft feel with abundant natural light.

Gensler Washington, DC, DatesWeiser XO Showroom, New York, 2000. A column penetrates a ceiling, and the resulting void produces both the semblance of a capital and a sense that the ceiling is hovering above. Ebonized wood-framed doors are set as a visual juxtaposition against highly polished white floors.

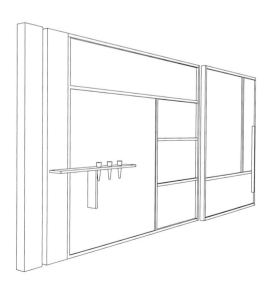

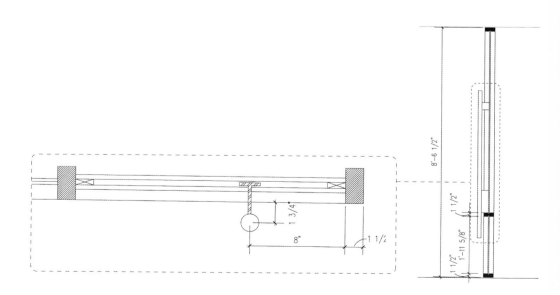

wall perspective

door detail

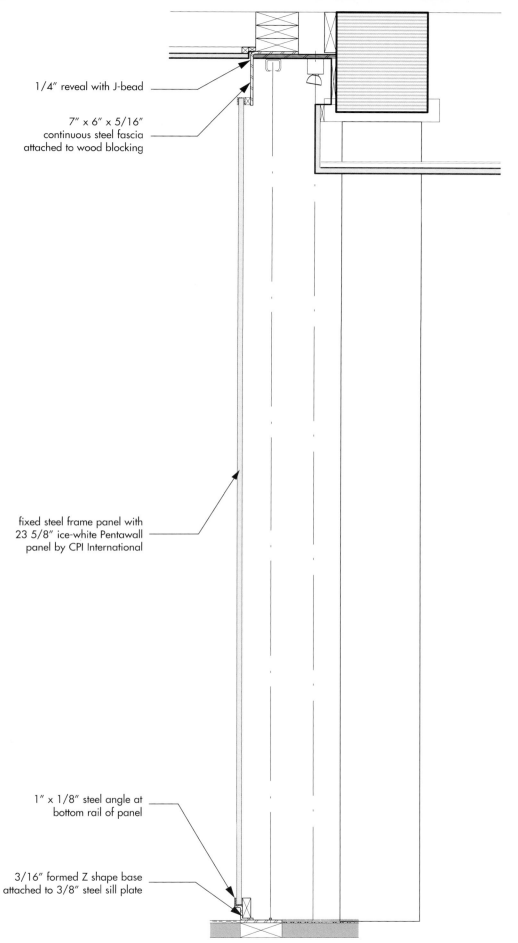

1/4" reveal with J-bead

7" x 6" x 5/16"
continuous steel fascia
attached to wood blocking

fixed steel frame panel with
23 5/8" ice-white Pentawall
panel by CPI International

1" x 1/8" steel angle at
bottom rail of panel

3/16" formed Z shape base
attached to 3/8" steel sill plate

Previous spread: Machado and Silvetti Associates, Lippincott & Margulies Corporate Offices, New York, 1998. Administrative workstations, storage, a pantry, and other service elements are contained in a volume wrapped in fiddleback anigre veneer with a horizontal coursing of limestone. Pivoting doors of individual offices are in two tones of frosted glass. This spread: Architecture Research Office, Capital Z Partners Offices, New York, 1998. Clear glass sliding doors trimmed in blackened steel retract behind screens of frosted plastic material. The glass doors are cantilevered and ride along single metal tracks that establish thresholds for each private office.

LOT/EK, Bohen Foundation, New York, 2001. An inventive arrangement of old marine shipping containers set on tracks lends this office a feeling of industrial authenticity while affording the occupants infinitely varying configurations based on their needs and moods.

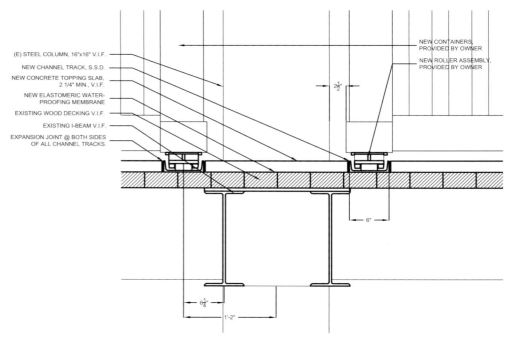

(E) STEEL COLUMN, 16"x16" V.I.F.

NEW CHANNEL TRACK, S.S.D.

NEW CONCRETE TOPPING SLAB, 2 1/4" MIN., V.I.F.

NEW ELASTOMERIC WATER-PROOFING MEMBRANE

EXISTING WOOD DECKING V.I.F.

EXISTING I-BEAM V.I.F.

EXPANSION JOINT @ BOTH SIDES OF ALL CHANNEL TRACKS.

NEW CONTAINERS, PROVIDED BY OWNER

NEW ROLLER ASSEMBLY, PROVIDED BY OWNER

new container tracks @ (E) steel columns   scale 1 1/2"= 1'-0"

retail

Architects who once might have dismissed retail design as too frivolous or less worthy of their talents now vie for commissions from the world's top merchants of glamour. ■ From pristine and spartan white spaces that have a monastic simplicity to bustling emporiums that seem to double as performance spaces, shopping is about more than furniture, clothing and other items. ■ The act of being out in the public marketplace is as vital a human need now as it was in the time of the Greek agora. ■ Poet Thom Gunn: "The shoppers bustled, bells rang without cease, you smelt a sharp excitement in the air . . . ."

Previous spread: Gabellini Associates, Jil Sander Boutique, San Francisco, 1996. This spread: Bohlin Cywinski Jackson, Apple Store SoHo, New York, 2002. At this "flagship" location, a structurally daring glass staircase is placed directly on axis to the store's entrance, a deliberate attempt to draw customers upward—always a challenge in retail. Adding to the enticement are a skylight above the stair and an etched-glass bridge that spans the two wings of the second floor. The elegant minimalist theme is continued with Pietra Serena stone floors and matte stainless-steel column wrappers.

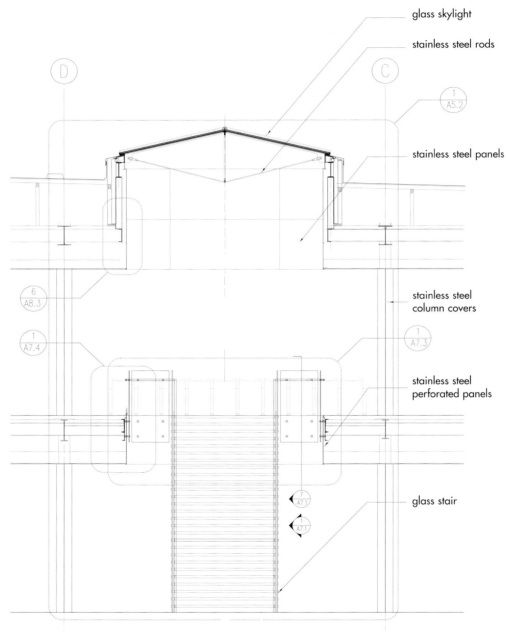

glass skylight

stainless steel rods

stainless steel panels

stainless steel
column covers

stainless steel
perforated panels

glass stair

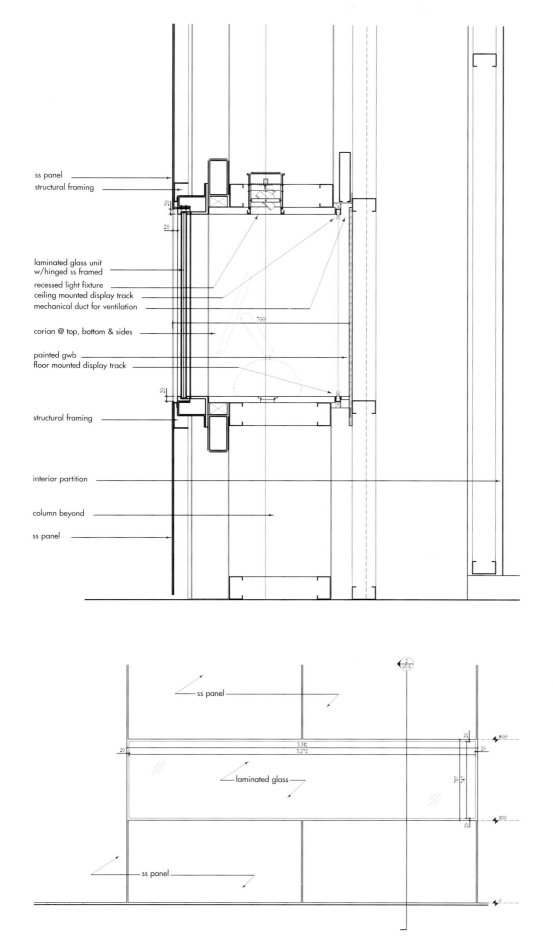

ss panel
structural framing

20
20

laminated glass unit
w/hinged ss framed
recessed light fixture
ceiling mounted display track
mechanical duct for ventilation

700

corian @ top, bottom & sides

painted gwb
floor mounted display track

20

structural framing

interior partition

column beyond

ss panel

ss panel

2
45-6

ss panel

20
20

3.312
3.272

787
747

1600

laminated glass

800

20

ss panel

0

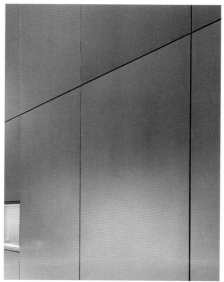

Bohlin Cywinski Jackson, Apple Store Tokyo, 2003. Precision manufacturing, perfect alignment and meticulous detailing mark the store's bead-blasted stainless steel panels.

This and previous spread: Gluckman Mayner Architects, Helmut Lang Store, New York, 1998. Display cases as minimalist sculpture: Monolithic black structures house the designer's collections. Items are hung on a single rod while being backlit to give a sense of the detail and artistry inherent in each.

John Pawson Architect, Calvin Klein, New York, 1995. As the designer's flagship store, this exercise in retail and design restraint gained attention in the mid-1990s as something of the apogee of minimalist chic. Glass railings, devoid of metal frames or other hardware, recall the "almost nothing" design dictum of Mies van der Rohe; light gray stone pavings are set in a precise grid of three-foot squares; light wood benches by artist Donald Judd offer a spot from which to survey the entire scene of restraint and tranquility.

Peter Marino + Assoc Architects, Chanel Store Paris, 2003. Before Coco Chanel, black was generally thought of a color of mourning. As if in tribute to her making this the most fashionable of colors, the architect employs vitrines in glass with black backgrounds, which set off the merchandise contained within. Key walls are perforated creating a pattern resembling computer punch cards and backlit.

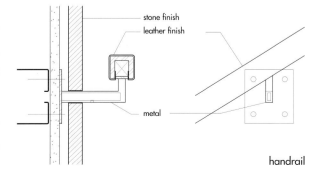

stone finish

leather finish

metal

handrail

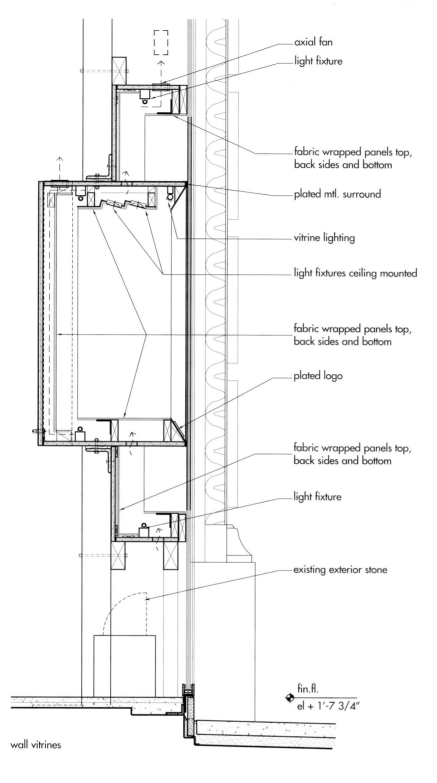

axial fan

light fixture

fabric wrapped panels top, back sides and bottom

plated mtl. surround

vitrine lighting

light fixtures ceiling mounted

fabric wrapped panels top, back sides and bottom

plated logo

fabric wrapped panels top, back sides and bottom

light fixture

existing exterior stone

fin.fl.
el + 1'-7 3/4"

wall vitrines

Peter Marino + Assoc Architects, Chanel Store Madison Avenue, New York, 2001. The iconic Chanel logo made the simplest black-and-white sans serif type the ultimate in simple luxury. In much the same way the architect here uses dramatic black regulating elements to organize and animate the space.

Peter Marino + Assoc Architects, Christian Dior, Beverly Hills, 2001. Engraved, laminated and hammered mirrored glass walls surround the store's cosmetics area and are arranged as carefully proportioned panels. Aimed at bringing in as much of the Southern California light as possible, a double-height glazed façade forms a dynamic and animated streetfront. This wall of glass and stainless steel has two notches cut into it for entrances and is counterbalanced by a single tree, set strategically off center.

exhibition

"For in a house that serves the Muses, there must be no lamentation: such a thing does not befit it."—The Greek poet Sappho. ■ The notion of the display and exhibition of art as some aristocratic pursuit has given way to a more democratic idea of museums and galleries whose displays can soothe and enlighten, but also question and challenge. ■ Some continue to insist on architecture as a "neutral" vessel for holding art; others see architecture and art as a symbiosis, each informing the other. ■ Writer James Cawthorn: "For him the muse shall wake her ev'ry art, exhibit truth, and open all the heart."

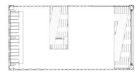

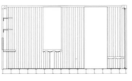

containers

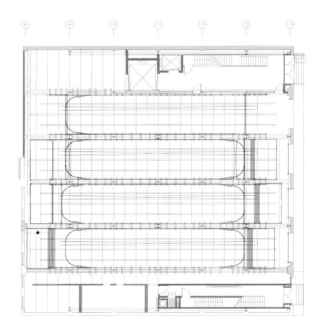

reflected ceiling

Previous spread: Gwathmey Siegel & Associates Architects, the International Center of Photography, New York, 2000. This spread: LOT/EK, Bohen Foundation, New York, 2001. In the office/gallery of a non-profit arts foundation, corrugated metal marine shipping containers are sliced into sections. Two of these units are placed along each of four sets of tracks in this industrial-style loft space. Curators can then slide the units to and fro, customizing spaces to fit the needs of a particular exhibition. White wall panels are also movable, thus allowing an almost infinite variety of interplay and interpenetration among the various elements.

sections

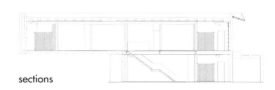

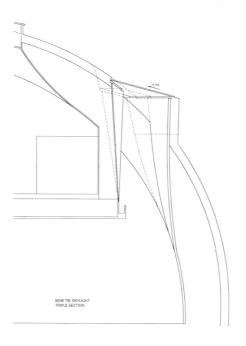

BOW TIE SKYLIGHT
TRIPLE-SECTION

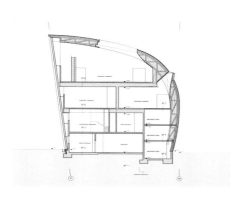

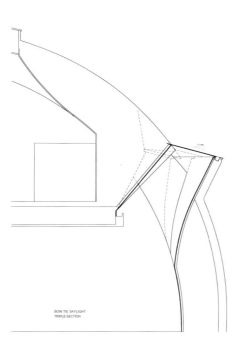

BOW TIE SKYLIGHT
TRIPLE-SECTION

Steven Holl Architects, Kiasma Museum, Helsinki, 1998. The individual galleries of the museum are designed to provide a quiet atmosphere in which the full intensity of the artwork can emerge, as in these spaces on the third floor on the east façade. But as equally important are the provision of natural light, and the connecting of the building to the city around it. An equestrian statue of weathered copper is seen through the precise black grid of window mullions.

Steven Holl Architects, Bellevue Art Museum, Bellevue, Washington, 2001. In the building's upper lobby, frosted and clear glass form the perimeter of the museum library. One of the galleries takes on a glacial appearence when its walls are left bare. The angular profile of this exhibition space contrasts with the curvilinear wall design found in other parts of the museum.

This and following spread: Bohlin Cywinski Jackson, Liberty Bell Center, Philadelphia, 2003. Multiple layers of support form the armatures for the exhibit panels, which were designed as an integral part of the building's architecture. The connections between stainless steel, frosted glass and painted aluminum are expressed and celebrated while demonstrating the method of their making. Alongside the exhibit area, an undulating granite wall directs visitors through the exhibit and on towards the Liberty Bell.

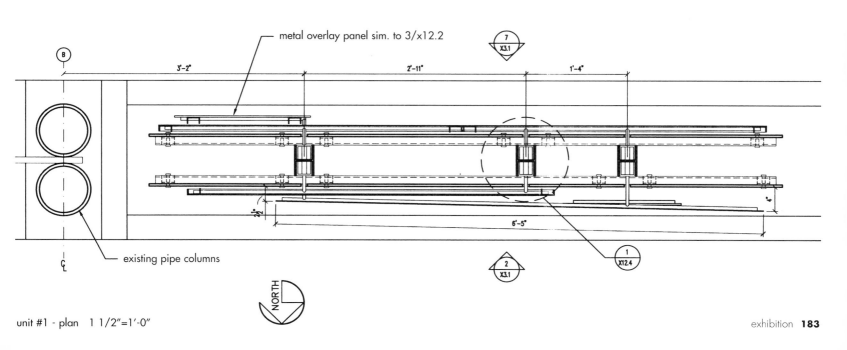

metal overlay panel sim. to 3/x12.2

existing pipe columns

unit #1 - plan   1 1/2"=1'-0"

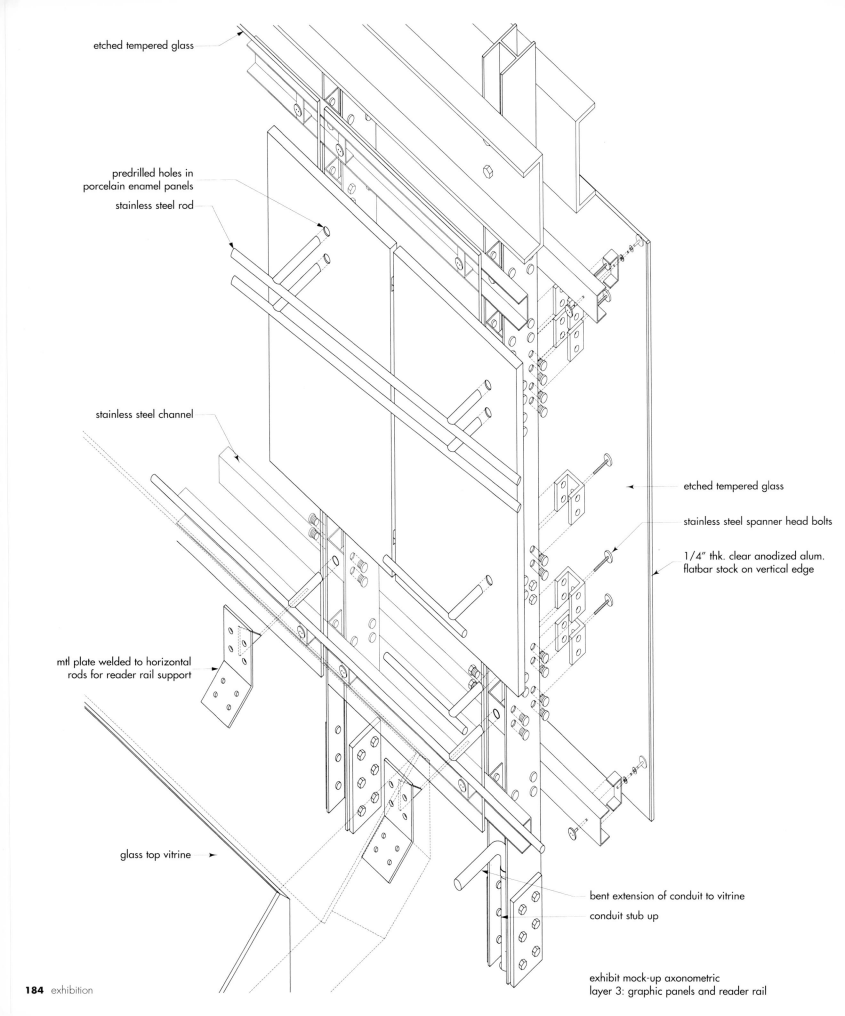

etched tempered glass

predrilled holes in
porcelain enamel panels

stainless steel rod

stainless steel channel

mtl plate welded to horizontal
rods for reader rail support

glass top vitrine

etched tempered glass

stainless steel spanner head bolts

1/4" thk. clear anodized alum.
flatbar stock on vertical edge

bent extension of conduit to vitrine

conduit stub up

exhibit mock-up axonometric
layer 3: graphic panels and reader rail

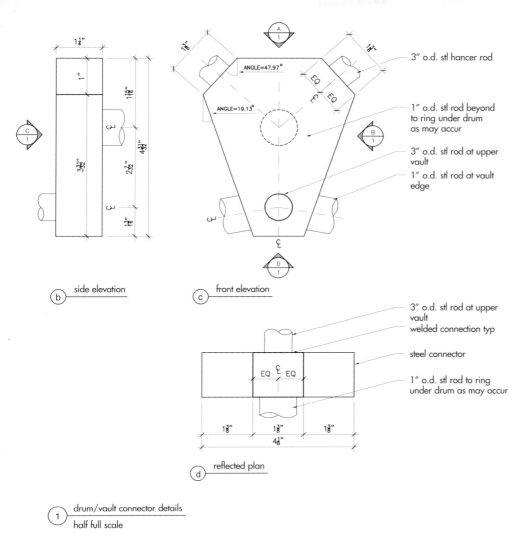

side elevation

3" o.d. stl hancer rod

1" o.d. stl rod beyond
to ring under drum
as may accur

3" o.d. stl rod at upper
vault

1" o.d. stl rod at vault
edge

ANGLE=47.97°

ANGLE=19.13°

EQ EQ

b — side elevation

c — front elevation

3" o.d. stl rod at upper
vault
welded connection typ

steel connector

1" o.d. stl rod to ring
under drum as may occur

EQ EQ

d — reflected plan

1 — drum/vault connector details
half full scale

This and previous spread: François de Menil, Architect, Byzantine Fresco Chapel Museum, Houston, 1997. Eschewing what would be a futile attempt to replicate Byzantine architecture, the architect chose instead to use an architectural language that would suggest the frescos' original setting. Thus four glass arches come together to form a vault, and the pendentives are suggested by the void left at the corners. The whiteness of the low-iron glass and the black void beyond provide an ideal neutral backdrop to this ancient iconography.

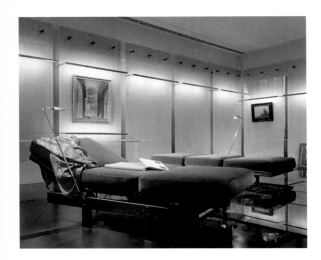

Parsons + Fernandez-Casteleiro Architects PC, Collector's Apartment, New York, 1993. For an art collector's three-room living space, a system of perforated aluminum panels allows flexible hanging of paintings; each panel has a low-voltage system for lighting. Flamed steel panel floors add to the sense of industrial chic. Furnishings include a motorized hospital bed and a sliding daybed on a curved aluminum track mounted to the floor.

We are indebted to a large number of people whose help was indispensable in the creation of this book. At Rockport Publishers, our appreciation extends to Ken Fund and Winnie Prentiss for their enormous and unconditional support, the trust they placed in us, and the creative freedoms they allowed. Special thanks for generously providing images and, in some cases, commentary at various stages of the book's development are due to Peter Bohlin, Michael F. Conner, Marika Simms, and Sterling Alexander from Bohlin Cywinski Jackson; Rosemary Suh from Peter L. Gluck and Partners; Gary L. Shoemaker, principal of Gary Shoemaker Architects PC; Adam Yarinsky and Kim Yao from Architecture Research Office LLP. To Mark Pasnik, and Lisa Pascarelli, we owe a substantial debt of gratitude for their willingness to be enlisted at the most strenuous moments of editing and production. Rodolfo Machado and Jorge Silvetti provided support without which this project would never have occurred. To Paul Warchol, who opened his extensive photography library to us, we cannot sufficiently express the appreciation and respect we feel for his work. During several trips to his studio and while sifting through thousands and thousands of images in his archives, we depended upon the kind support of Amy Barkow, Gabrielle Bendiner-Viani, Michele Convery, Bilyana Dimitrova, Devon Banks, and Ursula Warchol. And most of all, we are indebted to the creative forces behind the details we have showcased—a list of architects and designers too numerous to recount here. We thank each of them.

acknowledgments & dedications

In loving memory of my parents,
John D. and Eugenia S. McCown.—JMc

To Susan Parker for her endless friendship.—ORO